The Spiritual Practices of Creating Income

FOR ENTREPRENEURS, INTRAPRENEURS AND SOLOPRENEURS.

Bohemia
Press

Susan Lustenberger

Dedicated to

My amazing children, Jack, Lila and Maeve

and

My beautiful and brilliant sisters Mary, Tisa and Anne.

I love the six of you more than you will ever know.

Acknowledgement

This book could not have been written by me alone, it is the pioneers who have taught the Universal laws for hundreds of years that have paved the way for authors like me and the many more to come.

It is because of amazing visionaries like David R. Hawkins M.D., Ph.D, Masaru Emoto, Louise Hay and Rhonda Byrne who have created an awareness of truths that cannot been seen, but when believed and acted upon have the ability to change the world by magnatudes unmeasured. You have my unwaivering gratitude.

I am so grateful my kids, who have conversed with the top of my head because the rest of me was buried in my laptop for months. Who always ask with such enthusiasm "Whatchya working on?" and act surprised and delighted when, once again, I answer with "My book."

I am the luckiest woman in the world, I am.

Contents

Introduction

If you are reading this, something very special has just happened. You have been guided to look at a different way to go about creating success in your business. You might put this book down after reading this intro and go back to creating success through hard work, sleepless nights, and endless stress. That's okay if that is what you choose to do, but you don't have to.

In 2010, I came to a tangible realization that when we come from the place of joy, creation, and love, our success is easier and creates more prosperity. Let me spell it out for you: you make more money when you are happy. Keep reading, do what I suggest, and let me prove it to you.

If you work with me, know me, or are related to me, you know all too well that I am on a not so secret mission to change the world.

I believe that when we change where money comes from, we will change the world. So, I want to change where money comes from.

Obviously, there is the "duh factor" in what I just said. I am sure you briefly imagined that I meant the big banking industry, the national debt, or our seemingly dicey political affairs. Those are what I call the "duh factor," and while I truly believe that is the big picture outcome we need to change, that is not what I am talking to you about in this book.

What I am actually talking about is changing the belief system around money. One that takes you from the belief that creating success is hard, stressful, and exhausting to the belief that creating success and being happy and prosperous is your birthright. If it is your birthright like breathing, then it should be an endeavor that is easy, joyful and expansive.

As part of the wonderful collective of entrepreneurs, intrapreneurs, and solopreneurs, you are working an average of sixty hours a week. Actually, when you really add in all of the urgent moments that you take out your phone, write down thoughts and reminders, or wake up in the middle of the night remembering you needed to follow up with someone and then realize two hours have passed while you "just got a head start on your day," it's more like eighty hours week. We are a generation who has been raised with the belief that you have to work your fingers to the bone to make your business work. Yes, I said work, not succeed because as long as you are stuck in the limiting belief of work, the Universal Law of Attraction will deliver just that: more work.

Right now, people are more afraid than ever about their financial security, and that translates into overworked corporate cultures, eyes bleeding from exhaustive entrepreneurs, and the ever popular "no time for dreaming, so give up now" mindset. Somehow, we got a bit lost in the creation of our dreams and bought off on the scary belief that money is hard to come by, there isn't enough for everyone, and income, work, and happiness are not words that belong in the same sentence.

We are a culture that feels we have to sacrifice everything and leverage not only our bank accounts but also our emotional and spiritual reservoirs as well. This is because we have bought three really big lies.

The first lie is that there is a spiritual path and a nonspiritual path. I am here to tell you that the day your little, naked baby butt came into this life, you came in as a spirit in a body. So, every single one of us is spiritual just by being born! There is no elitist spiritual group that is better than any other group and gets into the VIP tent in heaven while the not-so-spiritual spirits are in the line that goes around the block, waiting to hang out with the cool kids.

Look, people who are seemingly more spiritual just have more of an interest in spirituality and consciousness than someone who has a passion for knitting or working out. It is just like most of us are born with legs, but not all of us are marathon runners.

The second lie is that spirituality, consciousness, and walking an enlightened path is only for after 6:00 pm and on the weekends. What I mean is that we get up in the morning, meditate, pray, drink our Kombucha, and then get in our car, drive to work, and move throughout the rest of our day in a swirl of stress, anxiety, and unconsciousness. We disconnect from our birthright to create what our birthright is. Confusing? Yes! These first two lies keep us completely confused and disconnected from the truth of our path.

The trick to living as a spirit in a body is to know that as you walk through your work day, you are aligned with the highest expression of joy, happiness, and love, which is spirituality. Yep, there it is: the big universal secret. The reason we are here is to live in the highest expression of joy, love, and happiness! Sorry if I spoiled the end, but since I did, let's get to it!

I am going to ask something very important of you while you read this book. Set aside ten minutes (twenty minutes in a perfect world) every single day for the next thirty days (even if you blow through this book in a day) and just be with yourself. We cannot live in the world as the highest expression of ourselves when we are rushing around and not making ourselves a priority. We just can't. So, please set about creating a sacred space where you can be quiet and undisturbed. Light a candle and get to know yourself. I promise that huge shadow in the corner that is so scary and has kept you from undistracted alone time isn't as big as it looks. You know what happens to the big scary shadow in the corner when you shine a flashlight on it? It disappears. Let me and this book be that flashlight for you. You are important, and your business is vital for the world. It started out as a dream for you, and that matters to me. So, here we go.

CHAPTER 1

You Are a Spirit in a Body, So Doesn't It Make Sense That Your Work Is a Spiritual Endeavor?

Just by being born into the beautiful body that is sitting here right now reading this and living in the world that you are, you are spiritual. My point here is that we are not a body with a soul, we are actually a spirit that is organized by a soul which animates the spirit in the human form giving us a personality, our laugh, our cry, the love we feel, and our happiness.

To make this easy, let's take the analogy of religion:

God, the universe, or your higher power is an expansive love energy this is infinite and cannot be measured. God has given words, belief structures, books, and communities through an organizational structure called religion. Then that religion gathers, speaks, and worships in what we call church. That is the breakdown of God, religion, and church.

Now here is the breakdown of us.

Spirit - The energy that passes from physical to non physical.
Vibration is the fastest.

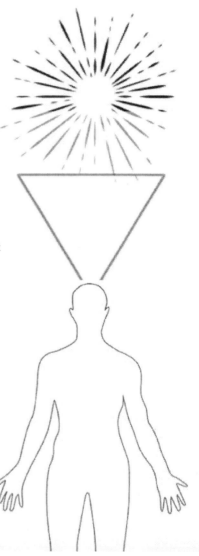

Soul - The organizational system for the spirit. Our personality, feelings, beliefs. What Dr.'s don't see when the cut you open. Vibration is second fastest.

Body - The vehicle that houses our soul, which holds and manifest our spirit into physical for, This vibration is the densest.

The Spirit is the all-being. It's the highest energy that we vibrate at. The spirit enters the organizational structure during an incarnation, and that structure gives us our personality, thoughts, emotions, and dreams once the spirit enters it. That's what makes up our soul. The soul, which vibrates at a slower rate than the spirit but at a higher rate than the body, then enters the body. Just like churches are the house of God, our bodies are the house of our spirit.

We do not say, "I am hand," or "I am heart." We say, "I have a hand," or "I have a heart." That is because the *I* is our spirit. So, we are all spiritual beings, and our work, being an extension of that, is always going to be a spiritual endeavor.

We are so lucky to live in a world where it is completely acceptable to work on your spirit as a strategy for creating business success. I have been working with executives, athletes, and business owners for a decade now and have seen the most amazing transformations in people and their businesses by focusing inward and creating happiness and prosperity spiritually.

When you live and create a business through consciousness and the awareness of your spirit, you align your brain with the vibration of your heart. When your brain and your heart are aligned, you are calibrating at love or joy, and that changes both your personal experience in all things and the world.

Our culture is changing, but up until recently, the consciousness around who we are was the awareness of our physical being. With the health and wellness industry being dominated mostly by beauty and anti-aging product sales of $679 billion, followed by fitness at $390 billion and healthy eating, nutrition and weight loss sales at $277 billion. These vast revenues show you just where our society has put the focus of our existence in this lifetime. Yet people are more rapidly becoming less satisfied, unhappy, and feeling more emptiness in their lives than ever before. This is because we are concentrating and putting our energy on the wrong things. We are focusing on the outside and our perception of success. But when we are aligned spiritually, everything becomes easy and prosperous.

Living Vibrations

700-1000	Enlightenment
600	Peace
540	Joy
500	Love
400	Reason
350	Acceptance
310	Willingness
250	Neutrality
200	Courage
175	Pride
150	Anger
125	Jealousy/Desire
100	Fear
75	Grief
50	Apathy
30	Guilt
20	Shame {self loathing}

**David Hawkins Power vs. Force

As spirits, we are energy, and energy is measured by vibrations. We each calibrate at our very own vibration, and we got that vibration from the household and family we grew up with. It is our baseline vibration, and we have had it since about seven years old. As we grow up and experience life, we edit our vibration, but we always have dominant attributes from that baseline calibration. Our calibrations are made up of beliefs whether they are limiting or not and emotions we have, judgments we make, and actions we take in the world. To shift those vibrations, we must keep our thoughts, beliefs, and actions crystal clear and healthy at all times. This can be a challenge if you have a low or fear-based baseline vibration.

In order to succeed in business, we must come to the spiritual being that we are. When we do, we cannot sit in a lower consciousness because we are not sitting in the ego.

I can hear you now saying, "Oh, no! Not another spiritual book about ditching, tricking, or killing the ego." Nope, this is not. You see, the ego is very important to the organizational system of the spirit. However, it is not the most important. My wisest advice to you would be to make your ego your new BFF. Why? Because anyone who is going to embark into the sometimes terrifying world of entrepreneurship has to have a good and healthy ego. Notice how I said *healthy*. Being in fear, competition, judgement, or insecurity is *not* healthy. But the joy of knowing that you have an important voice to be heard or knowing that you have created the most wonderful doohickey ever is exactly the support and cheerleading you need from your new BFF so that you can go out and take this world by storm. You need and should want a wonderfully aligned and balanced ego.

So, where does a spirit begin to create a successful and prosperous business? It begins with you and the awareness of the entrepreneurial consciousness you hold. Your entrepreneurial consciousness dictates the vibration your business is calibrating at. This is a crucial for you, the entrepreneur because this is where you can create and cultivate the clairvoyance you need around you, the spiritual being, and your business, the spiritual endeavor. Let's begin.

CHAPTER 2

The Four Entrepreneurial Consciousnesses: Creative, Competitive, Contracted, and Can't.

In business as in life, there is always a spectrum of degrees to which we lean. Nothing is black or white in consciousness because we are energy, and consciousness is the awareness of that energy. It is always changing, morphing, and—hopefully—elevating. In this chapter, I want to show you that on our journey here, we have the ability to transcend to higher, happier, and more abundant beings. The four entrepreneurial consciousnesses are a guide and reference point for you to have reflection, awareness, and a start on your journey with me through the pages of this book.

Before you read on, I want you to follow this link and take the entrepreneurial consciousness quiz to identify what you are. C'mon. I'll wait. You'll love it!

https://susanlustenberger.com/what-is-your-entrepreneurial-consciousness-quiz/

See, wasn't that enlightening and fun? Now that you have an idea of where you are, we get to look at the spectrum and where you can go. Remember, it's all a spectrum, and we are all supposed to blend and exist in the world of business together.

Creative Consciousness
Archetype: The Dreamer

Energetic belief structure:

1. There is more than enough for everyone.
2. If one succeeds, we all succeed.
3. The more I exhale prosperity, the more I succeed.
4. My industry is at one with me.
5. Dominant vibration: Love

You are a source of high vibration in the entrepreneurial world. Your dominant vibration is love, which calibrates at 500. It is said that 1 person calibrating at love, which is 500, transmutes 150,000 people calibrating at fear, which is 100. Whether you are an entrepreneur or intraprenuer, you bring all who are lucky enough to work with you into your elevated experience. When we come from the Creative Consciousness, the options for success are limitless. The universe conspires in your favor, and you, the Creative Consciousness, easily receive all things abundant and good. You are perfect partners in success.

Point of Acceleration:

Being inclusive of all people and situations to see what serves the best and highest good. Being open to the magic of opportunities that are aligned with your intuitive compass.

The Stall:

You can be way too distracted by possibilities (love the shiny, sparkly stuff). Money and income come easily to you, but by holding the tendency for distraction, you can easily miss what is right in front of you because you are looking at the beautiful scenery way up ahead.

Archetype: The Dreamer

At the core of who you are, you are a dreamer. The most powerful vibration dreamers hold is love, for when we sit in the vibration of love, dreams manifest into reality at the speed of light. As you hold yourself in this spiritual business space, you need to stand back to create clairvoyance around the business details and next steps. Focus on today's business at hand instead of creating the experience of a lifetime for all involved. You being a Creative Consciousness will manifest success and income for all without much effort. Focus, focus, focus!

This entrepreneurial consciousness thrives and loves being in the "in love" stage of their business. When everything is new and everyone is in the bliss of the newness, they are at their happiest. Often times, the Creative is the first one to bail on a project when things shift into taking action and moving the love affair into the marriage of the business and its day to day. The most powerful Creative is the one who has a smidgen of underlying Competitive Consciousness to keep them in the game, wanting to see the end result flourish and succeed.

I myself am a Creative with underlying Competitive energy, but it wasn't always that way. I used to believe that you could only be one or the other. When I was in Corporate America, I was competitive through and through. However, I would spend my weekends and evenings dreaming up projects and business models that I would dangle in front of my consciousness as the "I will do this one day" carrot.

I truly believed that for me to slip into my Creative Consciousness, I had to come from a really soft, flowy place within me, and for someone who had been a competitor in business, that felt horrible and not like me at all.

The result was that I would start amazing businesses as a creator and then one by one watch as they fizzled out due to my lost interest in "the game." It wasn't until I entered a competition to gain exposure for one of my business that that fire was lit within me, and I saw how vital and real the joy of competition was for me. I saw the importance of the balance of it all. I won the competition, and my business exploded into so much prosperity and abundance that I was forever changed. Now, I happily dwell as a Creative Consciousness with Competitive tendencies.

So many Creative's just can't muster competitive energy around anything. They range from not wanting to partake in the game to downright phobic and steeped in limiting beliefs that competition is bad. The Creative Consciousness that dwells within this reality needs to have a Competitor close at hand to help lend the energy to an action-driven business plan.

Competitive Consciousness
Archetype: The Warrior

Energetic belief structure:

1. In order to win, someone must lose.
2. There is not enough for everyone.
3. Me as opposed to we.
4. See their industry as separate from them.
5. Dominant vibration: Pride

You walk the tight wire of the high vibrating energy of the Creative Consciousness and the intense vibration of pride. Pride on the scale of vibrations calibrates at 175, which creates more stress than joy for the Competitive Consciousness entrepreneur. The Competitve Consciousness is the most powerful manifestor of all of the consciousnesses. When you positively anchor into the emotional energy you hold, there is nothing that you cannot achieve.

Point of Acceleration:

Always on your game and quick to take action. You are an achiever. When you focus on the powerful energy of your success, you are limitless!

The Stall:

Keeping your eyes off other people's success in comparison to your own. You are misguided by believing that success is limited to the win.

Archetype: The Warrior

At the core of who you are, you are a warrior. Most days you are a warrior of good, but unfortunately, you easily stray to the dark side of "win and lose." It is imperative to explore and incorporate the spiritual practices of creating income to keep you centered on what really matters. When you hold the awareness of what really matters, your competitive spirit shines so brightly that you will easily succeed beyond what you could imagine. You know that spiritual warrior is inside of you. Let it free and watch your prosperity explode!

The Competitive Consciousness is a force to be reckoned with. They are on the verge of a takeover at any given time. This can be a good thing or a bad thing depending on how far up or down they are on the spectrum of entrepreneurial consciousness.

The Competitive is by far the most common consciousness. Recently, I was speaking to a group of entrepreneurs, most of whom had taken the quiz before they attended my talk. When I made reference to the quiz, the attendees who signed up for my talk last minute and hadn't gotten the memo that there was a pre-workshop quiz all shot up their hands in a panic. I assured them that the quiz was permanently available on my site, and they could take it once they arrived back home from the conference. I actually told them not to take it until they got home and could center, focus, and have time to think and feel through the answers. Well, what do you think happened? Yep, before my talk was over, some had pulled up the quiz on their phones and taken it. All of them came back Competitive! This is a powerful and mighty entrepreneur.

Unfortunately, the majority of Competitive entrepreneurs believe that being a Creative is less powerful than their energy of competition. However, when a Competitive entrepreneur is actively working on upleveling and sliding up the scale to Creative Consciousness, they soon see that in expanding into intention and creation, they actually gain power. The power, however, feels so much easier and less stressful, and that is because the power isn't pushing and forcing. The power is allowing and joy. This works for the Competitive because they are still winning.

I worked with a gentleman named Tom a few years ago. He was an entrepreneur who had sold a few start-ups and was now a consultant for the tech industry. He was a delightful human being, loved by his community, a great dad and wonderful husband, and had a huge amount of friends, contacts, and support.

However, something was starting to go terribly wrong in his business, and it was affecting his personal life in a very negative way. He was starting to lose friends and the community support in his industry that he had always enjoyed. Colleagues were distancing themselves, and he was no longer getting the referrals that his business success was built upon. Additionally, his marriage was strained because his wife felt isolated by the fact that so many of their friends were becoming distant and estranged.

In getting to know him and learning about his life, it was clear that he was a competitor. His weekends were filled with triathlons and Crossfit competitions. It was when he was happiest.

I asked if I could go along with him during a day of meetings with his clients. We began our day with coffee and a review of each client that we would be visiting and spending time with. Some of these were friends of his as well. He was impeccable in keeping notes and reference points of each subsequent meeting. As I went over his files, something just didn't add up with what I was reading and what he said was happening.

By the end of the day, the problem was painfully clear to me, and it was a big one. Tom was fierce. As soon as we walked into the meetings, he became a completely different person. He became not just a competitor but a full-on warrior.

It was in these meetings that I realized that in order for Tom to believe he was succeeding and the client was moving forward to success, heads had to roll. He was going to war with really integral people on his path, and some were the same people who brought him on and created this opportunity to work together.

Tom was schooled in Corporate America Re-org's in the 80's and 90's. He believed that in order to make progress, you seek out the weakest link and get rid of them. There wasn't room in "his town" for both him and whom he deemed the problem. He couldn't for the life of him step into Creative Consciousness and see that he was creating such a cancer in the company he was consulting for and for himself. He had had such a success rate with all of his businesses back in the day that he just couldn't see past himself to shift into a higher way of being, and he was now doing business in a world that had long shifted out of the "heads are going to roll" paradigm. The word had gotten out about Tom, and both his professional and personal community had pulled away.

Tom wasn't ever able to make the shift. He closed up his business and took a high-paying corporate position back east. He and his wife moved and started over. Not everyone can make the shift, and sometimes, they can't make the shift right now. It is a choice, and when money is good, we often can't motivate ourselves to shift into great.

Contracted Consciousness
Archetype: The Saboteur

1. Struggles with not ever feeling ready.
2. Uses perfectionism as a delay to jump.
3. Looks at what's wrong, not what's right.
4. Focuses on others instead of self as a distraction or delay.
5. Dominant vibration: Envy/Desire

If you are a Contracted Consciousness, you struggle with the clairvoyance you need to trust yourself, those around you, and the universal forces at hand. Your dominant vibration is envy and desire, which calibrates at 125 and is far too low of a vibration to hold an amazing spirit as yourself and this magical path of business that you are on. You must look at what is right with the world, what you do, and who you are starting right now. While you have a competitive streak, you are different than the Competitive Consciousness because you see yourself on the outside of the game instead of engaged on the playing field.

Point of Acceleration:

Delivers with intentions and goodness for all! Is a huge supporter of colleagues, friends, and all who are aligned.

The Stall:

Perfectionism and OCCYTO: Obsessive, Compulsive Comparing Yourself to Others.

Archetype: The Saboteur

When you are critical of yourself, the universe simply delivers the mirror of your judgments. Inside, you know the truth of who you are and what you want to create in this lifetime. Your ideas and dreams are amazing, but you live within the prison of "What will others think?" and it paralyzes you. Aligning with the spiritual practices of creating income would center you on the truth of the success and prosperity you are put here for, which means no more sabotaging! You can go at your own speed toward success, so know that you are meant to experience ease, flow, and joy in all things. You are completely worthy of everything you want, and the universe wants to shower you with all the abundance that you dream of. Stop believing in only what you think you see and go beyond to what you feel. The spirit of who you are is right.

Imagine that Competitive Consciousness fell madly in love with Can't Consciousness, and they had a love child. The love child would be a Contracted Consciousness entrepreneur. The Contracted looks out into the world and sees the possibility of losing instead of the reality of winning.

The Contracted entrepreneur always notices what they are not doing right. They all predominantly suffer from Obsessive, Compulsive Comparing themselves to others. This is a prison of suffering and stalling because of the deep-rooted, limiting belief of not being good enough. They are the perfectionist of all consciousnesses. Perfectionism is their stall tactic, so they don't have to face the inevitable failure that they are convinced they are destined to experience.

The good news is that when a Contracted is flanked by both a Competitive and a Creative energy, they are easily able to shift and move into taking action and creating amazing endeavors. They excel at creating teams that can get things off the ground and into action. The Contracted is actually amazing in supporting a team of go-getters and creators. Things tend to get a bit dicey though when a Contracted finds themselves with too much time on their hands. The Contracted love conflict.

When everything seems to be going really well with a Contracted, they start to feel uncomfortable and out of control, and they create conflict. This comes from the limiting belief that success shouldn't be this easy. This makes them uncomfortable and also makes them question their legitimacy. The Contracted Consciousnesses need to feel like they have proven themselves worthy of success, and usually for this type of entrepreneur, that is hard work and stress.

Contracted also fall prey to seeing their industry and colleagues as a place to aspire to. In the theme of not feeling like they are enough, they don't actually see the reality of the success they have achieved. They are always pulling in the energy of other's success stories to compare themselves to, and they constantly feel left out and not included by their peers. This is a dangerous place to be, and it stems from not feeling "enough." When we are stuck in "not enough," we are coming from our ego. The ego is our dark little friend in the corner who is always trying to keep us not as happy as we are supposed to be.

If we are worried that somehow we are missing out on the fun or business opportunities, then we are dwelling in "Why not me?" energy, and when we live in the "Why not me?" energy, we are magnetizing more of it from the universe. The Contracted Consciousness entrepreneur must—and I mean *must*—immerse themselves in gratitude to turn this around in their life. When you are looking at what you don't have or are not included in, you are absolutely not sitting in gratitude. You can't hold both energies in your system. It's impossible.

Can't Consciousness
Archetype: The Child

1. I am; therefore, I can't (because it's hard).
2. Life happens to them, not created by them.
3. Paralyzed by 1 and 2.

4. Uses phrases like "I can't," "I don't know," and "I need."
5. Dominant vibration: Fear

There is good news and bad news with the Can't Consciousness. The bad news is that where you are right now feels horrible, and you feel paralyzed to make a change. The good news is actually great news, and it is that you are the easiest consciousness to create transformation through the spiritual practices of creating income! Your dominant vibration is fear, which is paralyzing, but have you ever heard the saying, "Good is the enemy of great"? Well, that is absolutely true. But since you struggle with being good, you can easily create great! The spiritual practices are made for you. In a world where you feel like you have tried everything, I assure you that you have not.

Point of Acceleration:

When beyond reason something goes incredibly well, they have a boost in their vibration level and easily create more success.

The Stall:

They can't get out of their own way with phrases like "I can't," "I don't know," and "It's difficult for me." They live in a world that happens to them instead of a world they create.

Archetype: The Child

The Child waits for others to make things better. They do not see their power in any situation. The spiritual practices of creating income are the structural framework that the Can't Consciousness needs to feel safe in the world of business. The Can't Consciousness needs to feel as if they are not working because as we all know, children don't work. The upside is that as a successful adult, you epitomize the playful entrepreneurial mindset that empowers the Can't Consciousness, and that is joy and fun. When the Can't Consciousness is having fun, the energy they create can light up the entire world. Remember, being spiritual is being happy, and who isn't happy when they are playing and having fun!

Believe it or not, the Can't Consciousness is the closest to the Creative Consciousness of any of the four. They just have two completely opposite vibrations. The Creative is love at 500 and Can't is fear at 100. They are both aligned with the same ideals.

However, the Can't believes that their success is unachievable because they either can't see it or have lived their life in the community of Can't. Can'ts almost always come from a long line of Can'ts, and they belong to a community of like-minded people who see the world as merely happening to them, and usually, what happens isn't great.

I call this the three C's of Can't: Choice, Contagion, and Community.

Choice:

Or should I say lack thereof? Can'ts live a life of "I have no choice." They are reactors as opposed to action takers, and they do not see the connection between their role and manifesting their dire outcomes. This is because they struggle to take responsibility for their life. I have found that this is almost always due to two extremes: they were endlessly blamed for things as a child and live in remorse, or they were never held responsible for anything good or bad. One way created a fear of looking at reality, and the other created a disconnect from reality. But both robbed the person of empowerment and desire to create their experiences.

Contagion:

You know what they say? Misery loves company! There is no truer motto for the Can't than that. Because the Can't lives in a world of suffering self-esteem and comparison, it is challenging at best and painful at worst to be around succeeding people. They seek out another Can't or find a Contracted who is struggling to raise their vibe, and they slowly weave themselves and their reality into the web of contagion. Have you ever had a really bad day and noticed how easy it was (even for you Creatives) to feel like nothing was going right? How easy is it for you to disconnect from the reality that you have created your current situation?

We all have it happen at one point or another. Now, imagine that was an everyday reality and that everything that you witnessed in the world from the time that you were a child supported your belief system. The Can'ts pain and struggle are real. The great news is that they are in the energy of desperation, and if you as an ally or boss stick with them and mentor them, they will make a shift sooner than Contracted and Competitive. Remember, good is the enemy of great. The Can't Consciousness doesn't experience much good, so they are easily moved up the ladder to great.

No matter where you are in the entrepreneurial spectrum of consciousness, the rest of this book will deliver awareness, practices, and new options for you to move forward and succeed. Whether you are a Creative in need of a landscape of organization to lay as a foundation or a Can't at the jumping point for the rest of your life, read on.

CHAPTER 3

Navigating Your Business Through Universal Laws and the Big Fat Lies We Tell Ourselves

I am often asked why I teach spiritual practice and the Universal Laws as a business strategy. The answer is because we are all spirits, and as vibrating, energetic beings, we exist through the energetic laws of the universe. This isn't airy fairy or ooga booga. This is quantum physics, and when we create a business with them as the foundation, we succeed at a faster and more sustainable rate. We are aligned and in the "flow."

However, most of us do not go about our day with the awareness of the Universal Laws. If that is the case for you, here are a few of the Universal Laws that are covered in the chapters of this book and are vital to the success of your new business paradigm.

A Breakdown of the Universal Laws

The Universal Law of Gratitude

> As you bless, you are blessed doubly. The Law of Gratitude says that for what you are thankful for, you will generate more of and more to be thankful for.

The Universal Law of Karma and the Law of One

> The more you give, the more you receive. The more you assist others, the more you assist yourself. The power of this law is fully realized in your day to day functions. Watch your motives!

The Universal Law of Fellowship or Gathering

> When two or more people with similar vibrations are gathered for a shared purpose, their combined energy directed to the attainment of that purpose is doubled, tripled, quadrupled, or more.

The Universal Law of Resistance

> That which you resist you draw to you, and you will perpetuate its influence on your life. "What we resist, persists."

The Universal Law of Abundance

> You have within yourself everything required to make your earthly incarnation a paradise if you choose to accept that which is your divine birthright. We live in a universe of abundance, although the majority of the population views it as the universe of scarcity. Just do not hang out with those types.

The Big Fat Lies We Tell Ourselves That Suck Out Our Energy

Lie one—I am too busy to have ease and flow. I will work on that when I have more time.

Truth—You are not, and no, you won't. What you are deeply attached to and centered on is busyness. Somewhere deep inside you, you have taken on the limiting belief that busy is how you justify your life. I am busy, therefore I am. Have you ever asked someone how they are only to be answered with a laundry list of everything they have to get done, how stressed they are, and oh my goodness, they are so busy? How did that feel? When we ask the question, "How are you?" we are asking, "How is your heart?" We don't mean, "Justify your existence to me."

Lie two—I don't know.

Truth—Yes, you do. You just either don't want to answer or don't want to take a moment to connect and find out (see lie one). This lie will detach you from your highest self faster than anything. When we say, "I don't know," we are passing on taking responsibility for our truth.

That phrase isn't allowed in my home. My kids were taught at a very early age that it wasn't a truth. When I ask, "Where do you want to go to dinner?" (and they hate that question) they have to either give me an answer or say that they don't want to make the choice. This is empowering to us because even saying that you do not want to answer connects us to truth, and in the connectedness of truth, we find answers.

Lie three—I can't.

Truth—Unless you are literally tied to a radiator or jailed behind bars, you can. You just don't want to. *Can't* is the verb of a victim. I know that sounds harsh, but here's the deal: *can't* is a knee-jerk reaction that protects us from having to take responsibility for what we want and don't want in the world. Nothing is more empowering than when you are asked to do something and say, "I don't want to do that at this time," or "I am unable to answer you right now, but I will."

A few years ago, I was repeatedly asked to go on girls trips with my friends. I was always saying, "I can't because of xyz," even though the truth was that I didn't want to. They kept asking, and I kept saying "I can't." They were getting annoyed, and I was starting to avoid them. One day, I told the truth, and it was okay! Yes, they were annoyed, but they got over it. I finally got to relax in the truth and empowerment of my own voice, and you can too!

Lie four—I need.

Truth—We only need air, water, food, and shelter. If it is something other than one of those things, then you want it, not need it! Need is steeped in lack consciousness. It says, "I am in survival mode, not flourishing mode." Yes, *need* is the easiest word to throw out when you see something that you love and adore or want a colleague to hit a deadline, but you don't need; you want. *Want* is one of those words that gives us the ability to claim our power and voice. To say, "I want something," says, "I am worthy of something." It may feel really uncomfortable at first. Try it for five days and see what happens. You will miraculously expand into the power of your spirit. Remember, the universe only delivers on want, not need.

Lie five—When I _____, then I will be happy! (I call this the "When I, Then I" disease.)

Truth—No, no, no! It never works that way! When we put conditions on our happiness, we reach our end result, are still ourselves inside, and that dream of being happy comes crashing down in a storm of disappointment. Do you know what we are disappointed in? That we are still us. When we come to a challenge with the mindset of "I am happy but want to create an upleveling in my life," we hit the jackpot.

I often tell people who want to move to start enjoying their home and pay attention to the details of it. Start having parties, redecorate, and be happy in the house they are currently in. When you are in that vibration of gratitude and joy, you set the intention to get an even better home in a better place. It miraculously happens!

So, when you say, "When I make $200,000..." or "When my company lands this account, I will be happy," you are coming from an energy that you are not happy right now. When you put stipulations on happiness, you get more of the stipulations, not happiness.

The bottom line is this, your life is now, not in the future and not in the past, it is right now. At any moment you can create exactly what it is you want, but you must know what it is that you want. The Universal laws are energetic forces that will support you in moving forward and acheiving your dreams. But, you have to show up and create the magnetic energy that can receive the gifts of prosperity.

When you look past the lies, limiting beliefs and negative self narratives, there is a world out there that is easy and fun. I believe that we stay in the stress and hard, because jumping off the happiness cliff is terrifying. We know what hard and stress looks like and we have manuevered it quite well, so why jump? Because, quite simply, in order to fly, you must jump. The Universe will always catch you.

CHAPTER 4

Cultivating Clairvoyance for Your Successful Business—Your Sixth Sense for Success

If I asked you, "What does your successful business look like?" how would you answer? Can you see every aspect of your success, both business and life in general, or do you only imagine your business and nothing else? This will define your ability to create success in your business.

If you don't know what your success looks like, you can't sit in the vibration of that and create it. If you can't visualize it, you cannot create it. If you can only imagine a successful business but not a successful life, you will create a successful business and a not so successful life. Sound familiar?

The remedy is easy when you focus on where you put the emphasis in your creation of this image. Where is your office? What does it look like? Who are the people around you? What are you wearing? Now, look at your friends, family, and community. Who are they? Now, look around your home. What is in it that would still be in your home when you achieve success? Really get a feel for what is surrounding you now that would be surrounding you in the future too.

Just like most important events in life, success must be planned for. You would never leave on a vacation and not know where you are going or what you will be doing when you get there. How would you know when you arrived? How would you know what to pack When we make the shift from employee to entrepreneur, we want to succeed, and in most cases, we can even imagine succeeding. However, we don't plan for it.

What I mean is that most of us try to be an entrepreneur on top of a life that looks like it did as an employee. You must create space in your life for entrepreneurship. Your life doesn't have to be an exhausting day to day hamster wheel of entrepreneurship. The habits of an entrepreneur are habits that reside in choice.

I am not saying that employees don't have choices. Some do, and some actually thrive as intrapreneurs in large companies. There is so much magic in that expansion. It's art.

Yes. I believe intrapreneurship is an art form. Do I believe that entrepreneurship is? No, entrepreneurship is an addiction, a lifestyle addiction, and we entrepreneurs wouldn't have it any other way.

Your Definition of Success

We are living in a world where we are bombarded with what success should look like, and while there has always been a social awareness of what the "cool kids" are doing, it has never been in such epidemic proportions. With the era of social media, we live in a constant state of lifestyle imagery and social status.

The most freeing moment is when you realize what *your* success is, not the internet's, Facebook's, neighbors', or spouse's definition is. It is the moment when you have true alignment of who you are, what you love, and what brings you joy.

So many people come to me, and they have no idea what brings them joy or what they love. These are basics in self-awareness. As we grow up and become an adult, we tend to put the things that give us joy on a shelf to come back to later. The problem is that when we do that and go about creating a life of jobs, business, families, and obligations without that part of us, we forget where that damn shelf was.

It is in the time spent alone with the intention of finding our definitions of love, joy, and success that the shelf emerges. One of the ways to bring yourself back to the awareness of your joy is to immerse yourself in the history of your joy. When you do so for a long period of time, your muscle memory begins to remember what it felt like to vibrate at that frequency, and you find joy.

I give my clients the following as homework and am always so thrilled when I get that random and joyous phone call when they come out of their "adulting coma" and remember what created fun, happiness, and joy for them in their lives.

Take out a pad of paper, light a candle, and put on music that you loved as a teenager or preteen. Now, I want you to write down "five years old," and then under that, write four or five things that made you really happy at five. Then grow up on paper five years and make a list under "ten years old" of four or five things that made you really happy at ten. Then you grow up every five years until you are the age you are now and make your list of four or five joys under each age. *Pow!* You just created a history book of your happiness and joy!

Now, think about you today and what brings you joy now. Not anyone else, just you. Now, keep this list in a place where you see it every day, and when you look at it, make sure you pull the emotions up surrounding the experiences that you have written down. This flexes that happiness muscle memory and builds up your vibration to joy. The vibration of joy is where amazing things occur in your life, and if you are running a business in the vibration of joy, you will create many experiences to be joyful about.

Here is where it all comes together in defining your success. Success is being surrounded with everything that brings you prosperity in joy, love, health, and wealth. Simple, right? You would think so, but so many of us look to what is parked in our neighbor's driveway or where our friend's kids are going to college or the latest barrage of success stories on social media, and suddenly, that inner wealth of knowledge fades into muffled sounds of atrophying truth.

Creating Your Plan and Habits of Success

Remember earlier when I asked you to visualize your perfect life? Well, now I want you to imagine your perfect amazingly successful business day. Pull out your notebook and start writing a list of what you see down to the last detail. As a successful business owner and income creator, what are you doing? What habits are you creating, and what habits have you let go of? What is your mindset as a highly successful entrepreneur?

Yes, to the different degrees that we have business and successful business owners, we have success mindsets that get us to the level we set out to achieve. You can't achieve global success if your mindset is stuck on "just getting by" or "a little local business." It just doesn't work. As we step into the success of who we are, we need to create a mindset that supports us in all the endeavors that we set out to experience. You will never meet Sir Richard Branson or Oprah if you never leave your home office.

Now that you have created your list of success details and attributes, write down the habits of each successful attribute. This creates your blueprint of success habits.

Back when time management systems were getting big, I had an amazing boss who taught me one of the most important life skills in the care of humans, and he did it through the dreaded sales cold call. He used to walk up and down the halls of the sales office saying, "I don't want to be able to tell if you are on the phone with a client, your best friend, or your mom." What he meant was that you better have the same positive, fun energy while selling to your clients than you do planning a night out with your best friend, and you better be as sweet and respectful to a client as you would when speaking to your mom. That is the amazing skill of creating an authentic connection.

The same boss used to have us build personal calls into our time management systems. He believed that for every three sales calls, you should hop on a personal call with a friend or family member for the same amount of time. He firmly believed that this kept up the energy of fun and relaxation. That was far before creating vibrations and the law of attraction was a thing. But he was right, and we were an extremely successful sales force.

The next awareness I want you to have is who you are surrounded by as a successful entrepreneur and who has left the picture that you have formed in your mind. This visual is a huge indicator of what your intuition is trying to tell you about who you should surround yourself with. We are so sentimental, and sometimes we keep people in our lives for all of the wrong reasons. We feel like it would crush them, or we don't want to rock the boat. But here is the thing: they deserve to move on and get either a better job, a better friend, or a better colleague. You aren't doing them any favors. When you keep people who no longer serve you around, you are keeping them from their highest expression of who they are and the joy they are here to create. Remember the Can't Consciousness and the Community of Can't? We keep people around us who are keeping us in lower vibrations just because we don't change. If you want to change, you must change!

CHAPTER 5

Creating Sacred and Intimate Business Relationships

Business Intimacy: It's Real, It's Sexy, and It's Your Ultimate Income Creation Superpower

That fastest way to create business intimacy is to have off the charts stellar work ethics. I say this because from the time we have our first job and as we climb the latter to success, our work ethics define us and the business that we succeed or don't succeed at.

My dad had a few steadfast rules, but the one rule that dictated my father's business and business relationships was "If you wouldn't sit down and have a cup of coffee with them, do not take their money!" Seems pretty easy, huh? Well, not so much if you are an entrepreneur who is just starting your own business and don't have a strong intuitive compass to follow. Things can get pretty dicey when money starts to become the motivation for business. If you are in the business you are in only to make money, do yourself a favor and get out now. You're meant for a life of so much more, I promise.

If you are in the business just to make money, you will never—and I mean *never*—make enough money to make you happy and successful. Because when we only have our eyes on the money, this crazy vibration sneaks in, and it says, "There is never enough." Before you know it, you are only focused on the sales that didn't happen and the contracts that didn't get signed . It's a vicious cycle, and there is no way out. Remember, what we put our attention on grows, so you really don't want to be focusing on the "nots."

When we are creating our business and going out and getting the business, we must remember that just like us, our clients are human beings. They are not their company, their job, or their budget. They are spiritual beings, and our work is, therefore, spiritually intimate.

What I mean by that is if someone has reached out to you for help or hired you to help them as an employee, then they are being vulnerable, and when you agree to help someone, that union is intimate. That is what you want! It is hard for people to ask for help even in business, so one of the most important actions you can take is to create a space in which they want to ask you for help. When you can create business intimacy between you and your new client, that is a bond that doesn't get cut when budgets do or when the newest shiny entrepreneur comes knocking on your client's door. So, how do you create business intimacy?

Well, you first create human intimacy carefully. No, not cautiously. *Carefully.* I mean you create a relationship that is created from caring. I am sure that when you created your business, when you were sitting and dreamily plotting it out, you thought or imagined yourself interacting with clients. What did you see? Did you just see the sale being made or contract getting signed? Or did you think about the people whom you were sitting across from, the people who had come to you and asked for help? Who were they? What did you like about them? What about them made you want to help them? These are just a few of the amazing "full of care" questions that can help you become intimately aware of the person you are doing business with. Who is your ideal client? If you are sitting there thinking "I really don't know," then it's time to figure it out.

The Law of Attraction: Like Attracts Like As a Business Model

The Universal Laws are what the spiritual practices are built upon. Most of us go out and buy one business book after another. However, we would be so much better suited for creating success if we lived through the knowledge of the Universal Laws.

Without a doubt, the most important one in this book is the Law of Attraction. As business models go, the Law of Attraction is actually the magic that happens when you do create clairvoyance around your business. The Law of Attraction says that like attracts like. For instance, if you are a business owner who has specific values and philosophies, you will attract clients with similar values and philosophies. The only way to break this rule is to take clients who are not aligned with you. They won't show up often, but they will show up. Be aware that working with unaligned people and businesses does not serve you or the success of your business.

CHAPTER 6

The Three Prosperity Chambers of the Business Heart

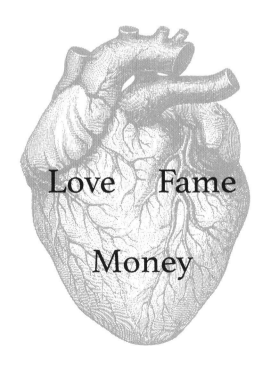

Love   Fame

Money

Each business that exists in the world has a center point. Whether you sell widgets or run a multibillion-dollar tech company, there is a center. Some see it as sales, some see it as operations, and others see it as the employees who work at the company. A very clear way of creating a success strategy with both clients and employees is with the Business Heart.

In the world of acquiring and retaining clients, sales is the prosperity heartbeat of our companies. We spend more money on sales forces, sales funnels, sales software, and sales training than we do on almost all other parts of our businesses combined. It is not who and how many accounts you acquire but the reason why you acquire that business that will create your success for both you and the client, and it will ultimately keep you in the game longer with much more sustainable prosperity and success.

There are two different entrepreneurial awarenesses that we tend to exist in. We exist in the awareness that we are in business either to make money or to create prosperity in our lives and the lives of the people we love. When we have the predominant awareness that we are in the business to make money, that is usually to create a life that we want to live. However, we are still focusing on the money, and as I said before, that can be a slippery slope. Being in business for money is extremely limiting and creates a contraction around other areas of abundance in our lives.

When we seek to create a life of prosperity, we expand into the energy of possibilities and that there are so many ways to prosper and make money from our businesses and the clients who come to us. Money is only one of the ways we prosper.

When you take a moment and think about each of the awarenesses, how do you feel? Which one sounds better to you?

We are moving to a different way to acquire business, and it's so much more intuitive and connected to the people who need us or our product. It's called the Business Heart.

The Three Rules of The Business Heart

Each Business Heart is made up of three prosperity chambers: Love, Fame, and Financial. The three chambers of the Business Heart is a framework that when followed, it will create aligned and sustainable success for you and your business. There are three rules when using this framework.

Rule 1: When you are soliciting a client or making contract decisions, your potential client must fulfill two chambers of the Business Heart.

Rule 2: One of those chambers must—and I do mean must—always be love. Yes, you heard me right. Love. It is actually the first and most important chamber of the Business Heart. When you are looking at new business or growing existing business, you must consider how you feel about these people or companies. If you do not in some way love them, love what they stand for, or love the experience of having them as a client, then you just don't solicit or keep them.

Rule 3: Each chamber has its own set of rules.

Love Chamber

The Love Chamber is the first and most important chamber of the Business Heart. It is where we look at the truth of who and how we are helping. It's the chamber that keeps us aligned with the integrity of who we are as a business owner.

Take a moment and think about your clients. If they weren't paying you, would you spend time with them? Would you have a cup of coffee with them just because? If the answer is no, then I would ask you to rethink your motivation in working with this client. We don't always have to love the individual, but we do have to love what the company stands for or what impact they are making in the world. There are plenty of personalities that just don't mix, but if you can see beyond the individual and sincerely get behind and want to be part of their belief system, then that qualifies them in the Love Chamber.

One of the most common disconnects is the disconnection of the awareness that our clients are vulnerable. When clients come to you, they are saying, "I have a deficiency, and I need your help." That is a very vulnerable moment. We tend to see it as a business opportunity, but we need to see it as a vulnerable human being asking for your help, not an opportunity for your bank account.

When we work with clients who do not fulfill the Love Chamber, it is exhausting. Have you ever noticed the difference in your energy when you spend the day with clients whom you love and are inspired by verses clients whom you don't? In living in our highest expression of expansion, it is imperative that we take care of our energy, and that means keeping our energy elevated, not exhausted. At the end of this book, there is an exercise that will help you gain clarity around your clients.

It goes both ways. If you are not feeling your best about a work relationship or you spend all morning hoping that your client cancels their appointment, you are not helping them. The energy of that is extremely exhausting and negative and will only cause lower vibrations and energy between you and your client, and that will not help. Remember, your clients are vulnerable. Don't be that person who takes advantage of that vulnerability just because you are not honoring the Love Chamber of the Business Heart.

Fame Chamber

The income and prosperity you generate from the Fame Chamber is that of universal energy and compensation.

When I say fame, I define that by a company or person who brings your business notoriety. This is okay. Really it is, especially when you lead with the Love Chamber. When you combine the Fame and Love Chambers, you are aligning with goodness. When you are aligned with goodness, both you and your client prosper in even more goodness. Here is a story detailing how powerful the Love and Fame Chambers are.

Many years ago, I was a corporate sales manager for a hotel in Los Angeles and the film studio mecca, Culver City. As a corporate sales manager, I was responsible for both the corporate market segment and the movie studio industry. I handled all frequent travelers from movie studios and corporate businesses in the area. These clients got an incredibly reduced rate with the hotel because they required a large number of room nights every month.

In the midst of all of the huge movie studios like Sony Pictures Entertainment and Paramount Pictures, there was a little tiny production studio with a new TV series out called *Baywatch*.

As a sales manager, I was thrilled to solicit this business. Unlike the huge movie studios, these people were amazing and fun to be around. While sales managers were saying they were on sales calls and going out to get lunches or manicures, I was saying I was on sales calls and going to hang out at *Baywatch* in their little bohemian surf style production hangar with some of the people who had become friends.

My boss wasn't so thrilled. *Baywatch* was pretty new and hadn't exploded off the charts yet, so they wanted to buy the best rooms for their guest stars but at a cheaper price. I convinced my boss to give the account ninety days, and I would prove to him that I could drive revenues up in other segments by doing this. He agreed.

What he didn't know was that whenever I was meeting with my corporate clients, the most asked question was "Do movie stars ever stay here?" When I could answer with "Yes, *Baywatch* is my best client," (They were my clients because they were my friends. Hello, Love Chamber!) *bam*, our rooms could have been tents out in the alley, and we would have had a new corporate client. That quarter, we were able to drive revenue over double of what we forecasted.

Baywatch became a permanent contract for the hotel, and even when they did explode in TV ratings and had higher travel budgets, we kept their rate the same. Because we treated them with love and care, they stayed with us when they could have easily gone down the street to the Ritz Carlton. Love and Fame are so powerful for creating prosperity for all.

It goes the other way too. Sometimes, it's the actions of our entrepreneurial spirits that create the fame for us and our client's benefit. TOMS shoes is a wonderful example of the later.

Blake Mycoskie is the wonderfully spirited entrepreneur behind the magnificent and generous global movement that started as TOMS shoes. He has generously given over sixty million pairs of shoes to children worldwide since 2006. He has also restored sight via TOMS glasses to 400,000 since 2011 and provided safe water for 335,000 weeks via TOMS Roasting Company from 2014–2015.

So, now when you purchase and wear a pair of TOMS shoes, you have garnered a bit of that philanthropic fame. You, the customer, are now associated with being in alignment with generosity and magnificence. This is a perfect example of aligning with goodness and goodness coming to you.

Now, look at your business. What goodness are you aligning with? What other goodness has it brought to you?

Money Chamber

The final prosperity chamber is Financial. It seems pretty obvious, but you would be surprised how many people really have a hard time with the concept of saying out loud, "I want money," even if they are providing a service or product for that money. I cannot tell you how many times I have asked people at events why they do what they do, only to be told, "I want to help others," "I want to give back to the world," or "I want to make a difference." Well, of course you do! But the truth is that you want to get paid for doing it! That is why you have created this business...to get paid for it, and it's okay. It's better than okay. It's great! If you are lucky enough to have created or work in a business that is your dream, then you deserve to get paid for it because you are probably very, very good at it, and that is good for the world vibrationally. Remember that in the vibration chart in chapter 1, the higher on that vibration chart you are, the better it is for the world. Although income isn't represented on the chart, it sure does lend itself for us to be, at the very least, neutral and safe, and that is a great place to come from when doing the work of creating spiritual practices in your business.

The Money Chamber might not always be the most important chamber for you in creating new business and bringing in new clients, but it has to be a priority at least half of the time because you have to pay your bills and take care of business. When I say take care of business, I do not mean roll up your sleeves and get to work. I mean you must be caring for your business, and when you are caring for something that is dear to you, that means that you must provide for it financially as well as emotionally and mentally. I know that you would not have gone through everything you have to make this dream come true if you did not care for it, so you must financially provide for it. That is the motivation coming from your Money Chamber.

By now, you have created a plan for cultivating clairvoyance around your business and created the practice of attracting your perfect client. When you stay on course with these practices by setting strong intentions, doing visualizations, and being impeccable in your motives for business, the financial aspect just magically falls into place.

So, remember, the sacred rule of the Business Heart is that you must always lead with two chambers of the Business Heart, and one must always be Love. You will never go wrong, and the universe will send you amazing clients and partnerships to fill your business with prosperity and abundance in all things.

As you find yourself humming along and receiving new and wonderful clients, it is often no time at all before you find yourself overwhelmed with all of the business that you are manifesting. To make matters worse, when you are in the new stages of building your business and creating your framework, it is very easy to create business upon trade, discount offerings, and freebies.

I had a client named Sheila come to me a few years ago, and she was so excited by how busy she was and how much money her new company was making. She was already working on her next year's forecast, and things were looking amazing. But in January, when she was having her taxes done, she hadn't made even close to what she thought. We conducted an energy audit of her time, money, and calendar, and she soon realized that her billable hours were taken up by networking calls, trades with other new entrepreneurs, discounted clients, and people who she had extended free offers to. She had almost run her company into the ground by being busy.

A few lessons were gleaned. The first being that she had to create a clearer consciousness around her income immediately, and the second was that she had to incorporate the framework called the Prosperity Pyramid.

Which leads us to one of the most important practices in your business.

The Art of Inhaling and Exhaling Prosperity—The Prosperity Pyramid

We cannot sustain life unless we both inhale and exhale. Money is the exact same energy as our life force. Money is our prana, our earthly life force energy.

We must exhale to inhale. Here is the exercise: I want you to take in a deep breath, and *do not* let it out. Without exhaling, take in some more air. Still don't exhale. Now, take in some more...and some more. At some point, you should feel like your lungs are going to explode. You may breathe now. In business, if we are only focused on the income that we are creating and not exhaling prosperity into the world, we will soon find ourselves unable to sustain our business life force. As the old saying goes, "You need to spend money to make money." When I created the Prosperity Pyramid, I had this principle in mind.

The Prosperity Pyramid is a quick glance framework to give you a clear sense of what type of business you are willing to spend your time on and a strong set of boundaries to follow to protect your time so that you can create the successful business that you dreamed of creating.

Free/Give

Here is the single most spiritual practice that you should be starting your business out with: always lead with give! Yes, always lead with what you are giving away to the world for free. Always give to people who hold absolutely nothing for you but to receive. If you tell me that you are giving away free videos, I am going to tell you that that is marketing. I mean take what you do in the world and find one person or one company to do it for completely free, or if it's a product, give it away.

I pick one person every single year, and I send them a lovely letter before the New Year telling them that for the entire year ahead, they get anything and everything that I offer as a gift from me. All I ask in return is that they just receive it. Some take me up on it. Some do not, but they know that it is there for them at any point if they decide to.

The other way to give, which is without a doubt my favorite, is to gift to a competitor and prospective client the gift of each other. This can only really be done if you are coming from creative consciousness and not competitive consciousness.

I want you to find someone or a company that does what you do, whether they are newer at it, have less overhead, or charge less than you. Then the next time someone calls you and for whatever reason you find yourself not wanting to work with them, whether they can't afford your rate, you don't have enough time for them, and they need you pronto, or you just don't have the same energy or vibration (and that is okay), send them over to your competitor. Yes! Gift away the business.

A few years ago, I had a woman call me, and she desperately "needed" to see me. She was very disappointed that she couldn't get an appointment for a few weeks but was willing to book the appointment and go on a waiting list for an earlier time. She asked me my rates, and when I told her, she asked me if I could discount her rate to one she could afford. I did something better.

I contacted another medium in the area and asked her if she had time right away to fit in this client. She could and was more than willing to accommodate the client at the rate the woman could pay. I emailed the woman and told her I was connecting her with another medium in the area who was just as good, had availability, and was happy to extend a rate that the woman was comfortable paying. The prospective client was thrilled, my competitor was thrilled, and I was more than thrilled because I was giving freely to two people in the world, asking nothing in return. That is the top and most important portion of my Prosperity Pyramid. When you follow your prosperity pyramid, you *prosper*!

You are probably wondering why I wouldn't just make it work for the prospective client. When I developed the Prosperity Pyramid, it was because I was having difficulties with boundaries. A very smart and wonderful friend of mine, Emiliya Zhivotovskaya, founder of the Flourishing Center, once gave me the advice, "Boundaries are the pillars to authenticity." At the time, that didn't make sense to me, but she was right. When I really gained clarity around that mantra, I saw all the ways I was not being authentic in my life and in my business. When you continually pack your week's schedule with clients and continually offer discounts or trades but have contraction or resentment around that business practice, you are not doing anyone any good at all. You are not being authentic.

In creating the Prosperity Pyramid, I laid out exactly what my commitment was to the kind of work I was doing in the world. When I first opened my practice, I, just like most baby entrepreneurs, was giving, trading, and discounting my business. I was ignoring my business and creating busyness.

In becoming clear on creating my boundaries, I also became clear on my hours and pricing of business and, most important, my business authenticity. I truly didn't have the time to fit the prospective client in, and I have very clear parameters around extending discounts. So, had I taken her on, I would not have done so without compromising my authenticity and negatively effecting the job that she needed done from me. To give her away was the highest form of care and customer service I could have engaged in.

Trade

The second level of the Prosperity Pyramid is trade. Trade has been around for centuries. There are still entire communities today that exist almost entirely on barter systems. There are over fifty barter and trade websites, and even Craigslist's trade section has become one of its fastest growing community resources.

Trading and bartering is a culture for some, and the people who align with this culture actually feel much more abundant with the currency of trade. They love the experience of the exchange of energy with trade, and that in and of itself is prosperous for them.

However, in this book and in creating your spiritual practices and Prosperity Pyramid, the topic of trade is much different. The reason trade holds the second layer of the pyramid is not because of its divine spiritual vibration but because trade relationships should be kept to an absolute minimum in the world of energy and vibration. On the prosperity scale of vibration, trade is actually one of the lowest forms of currency. Giving away is more prosperous than negotiating a trade of services. There are some exceptions such as the communities mentioned above, but trade comes from a haggling or lack consciousness. Trade energy and vibration is slow and unclear. It puts limitations on what you are willing to receive. Now, that is not to say that when you are starting your business and someone has what you need and you have what they need that you shouldn't help each other out. In some cases, it can be amazingly prosperous temporarily.

However, when you create an energy around accepting trade as currency, it is usually done because you cannot afford to pay for the services needed. That is completely understandable, but be really clear that when you set up this energy in your business, you are literally attracting people who cannot pay for your services either. This is the fastest way to find your phone ringing off the hook with prospective clients who cannot pay you and offer up trade instead. As I said before, trade serves a purpose, but only temporarily.

In an interview with CNN on trading and bartering, SwapThing Founder and CEO Jessica Hardwick said, "I think a few years ago it was more for fun...But we've seen a real shift in the last year, and especially an increase in the last few months, where I think people are really doing it to get by."

As I said before, trade is a lack consciousness. Even when done for fun for too long, that lack consciousness takes over, and prosperity is completely shifted in your business and life.

Trade is also the currency of business owners who have trouble receiving. When someone offers up a freebie and you throw out "let's trade," you are cutting yourself off from receiving, and if you can't receive from an individual, you definitely can't receive from the universe. You cannot be successful if you are not ready too. No matter how hard you try, you will come up against wall after wall after wall. Receive the success the universe has in store for you.

So, when a vendor or service provider offers you up a gifted service or product, take it gratefully and abundantly, and then if at the end of whatever help, services, or product you received you are inspired to give something back as a gift of appreciation, perfect! Give away! Gifting holds a completely different energy than the action of a trade deal. Gifting says, "I am abundant and can afford to give away," and when you give away, the universe gives you more. That is prosperous!

The Silver Lining of Trade

So, why include trade at all in your Prosperity Pyramid? Well because in some cases, it is how you, as a creator of income, can exercise your muscle on negotiating relationships. I say this because the most important practice you engage in when you are trading is the negotiated details. Yes! You need to negotiate the trade relationship. Do not engage in any trade without a clear sense of when it starts, when it stops, and how it will be detailed between the two parties. Do not leave yourself open to a negative experience down the line because someone else thought your trade agreement meant something it did not. This bears repeating.

Do not engage in any trade without a clear sense of when it starts, when it stops, and how it will be detailed between the two parties.

Discount

The third and final top tier on the Prosperity Pyramid is discounts, the amazing way we show gratitude to family and friends or drive business during slow times. However, discounts and the expectation around discounts can be a slippery slope. That is because discounting is the most unconscious of the exhaling prosperity sections, and when you create something unconsciously, it creates resentment when it's cashed in.

It is better to not extend discounts at all than to unconsciously throw out a discount and not have a consciousness around why and to whom. Don't forget that it's *why* you discount that matters, not *that* you discount.

America's companies are built on the family and friends who helped support us in our growth. Almost all businesses today show gratitude for those supporters by offering friends and family discounts. This is a wonderful and brilliant way to say thank you and be supported by your community at the same time.

To really get awareness on this section, I want you to take a pad of paper and pen, and I want you to leave your office. Go find a beautiful place to sit in nature or somewhere where you can't be disturbed. I want you to think about each person who has helped you while you built this business. Maybe they connected you to amazing clients, maybe they picked up and fed your kids while you worked on the launch of a product, or maybe they were the person who would hold you or listen to you when you thought failure was inevitable. Don't leave a single person out.

Then create a visualization of you giving these wonderful people your goods or services at a discounted rate. Watch and feel yourself figuring out what that is. I don't necessarily mean the literal discount. I mean what is the reason behind your generosity, what is the gift you are bestowing on them and why them. Get really clear on what kind of people or situations warrant a discount from you and then take out a pen and write down your discount plan. Then sit in the joy of being in the generous vibration of choice!

My final thoughts on the three upper tiers:

Give freely and wholeheartedly and ask nothing in return ever. Trade cautiously but from the wonderful spirit of abundance and clarity. Discount with utter gratitude to the people who it feels wonderful to do so. When you are clear on these three levels, let's bring in some income!

Income

The last and largest tier of your prosperity pyramid is your income producing business. However your business is broken down, whether you sell tires or consulting, I am sure that you have a variety of offers. Snow tires or bike tires, hourly consulting or retainer based contracts, these are all wonderful and spiritual ways to bring in income and add to your life. The trick though is being really clear on what is going to support you in your new spiritual business of ease and flow and wild abundance.

Now that you are a business owner who sets intentions and creates your prosperous reality, you get to look at that carefully. Nope, I don't mean be cautious. I mean you get to be full of care when planning for your utter happiness and success. Here is where you get to pick your favorite part of the job to focus on. Once you get clear on the ways you bring in your income, list it in the order that you most want to spend your time doing it.

As you can see in my pyramid, I have four ways in which I bring in active income, private contracts, corporate retainers, speaking gigs, and mediumship readings. I have carefully assigned each channel with a number that reflects how many of those I am willing to do in the year for the best and highest good of my joy, abundance, and time management. I am so aligned with my pyramid because I was full of care when I created it. I aligned with what I was committed to and how I intended to create my income from using this spiritual practice. Your Prosperity Pyramid is a tool for you to keep on hand. Let it guide you and support you in bringing in income and clients.

When I began creating my Prosperity Pyramid, I would use it more as a market segment tool to go out and bring in business, but then something shifted as I used it and got clear around my intention of it. The business started coming to me faster and faster in each segment. In 2015, I had booked all of my long-term private and corporate clients by the first quarter. I am happy to say that in 2016, I had all of my contract clients booked by the second week of January. This leaves a tremendous amount of time for me to create and explore other channels in building my joyful and prosperous life.

Sit in a quiet place where you will be undisturbed for at least thirty minutes. Close your eyes and take three deep breaths in and three long exhales out. Now sit with what the Prosperity Pyramid for your business looks like. Imagine you prosperous, happy, and clear on what your business boundaries will look like. Begin to create, and may you have blessings of receiving and bestowing generosity in balance.

CHAPTER 8

Don't Do "The Hustle" Unless It's the "Love Hustle"!

The Hustle

Two years ago, I was on a Consciousness in Leadership retreat with my accountability partners in the Santa Cruz mountains. It was a lovely group of five of us in a mix of twenty-five thought leaders in Corporate America.

While we were there, my colleague Morgan got a job that she was in the running for. It was a pivotal career move for her. She was moving into the position of president for her company. The five of us decided that we were going to sneak off and take her to a celebratory dinner.

As the day was winding up, we were jumping into the cab. Another colleague, Michelle, had to pick something up at the front desk, so she had us go ahead. Michelle was a huge mover and shaker and had completely come into her own just recently. She had created her own consulting company, and the hustle that she had worked so hard perfecting was paying off.

As we were seated in the restaurant, we opted to wait to order food and drink until we all could sit together and celebrate with a toast. Michelle was definitely not on our heels as promised. A few of us texted her, and she said "I am on my way. Don't celebrate without me." After forty-five minutes, we went ahead without Michelle and ordered drinks and appetizers. Michelle came skidding in and took her seat just as the drinks were being served. She was going on and on about a new contact she had just met and had the nicest visit with in the lobby and would probably be working together in the near future.

Through big eyes and forced smiles, we raised our glasses to toast Morgan and the huge milestone of success she had just had. Michelle asked to do the honors and what she said left us all in complete shock. She raised a borrowed glass of water and said, "Morgan, we are so proud of you, and now that you are president, I would like to ask you to get be on board for some consulting work with your company." That was her toast.

The group fell silent, and a few of us took over and toasted to Morgan's accomplishments endlessly, gushing over how deserving she was and how proud we were. The night ended up being wonderful.

Both Morgan and Michelle went on to be successful in their careers. Morgan never brought on Michelle as a consultant, and they no longer have a personal relationship. Morgan has a full life surrounded by friends and accomplishments. Michelle, on the other hand, is still in the hustle and feeling left behind. The end perception on Michelle's part was that

Morgan had gotten her dream job and forgotten about all of the "little people" and, in doing so, dumped Michelle.

In reality, nothing was farther from the truth. Morgan had expanded in relationships and in her role as a leader in her company and community. She also expanded in clairvoyance of what no longer served her highest self and what she wanted to do for the world. Had Michelle not been caught up in the hustle of it all, things probably would have turned out differently.

Holding and creating sacred space with the people around you is essential when you are creating a business of helping. Treat everyone with a sense of sacredness. You never know who your next client will be.

The Vibration of the Hustle—When we vibrate at "the Hustle," we get more of the hustle. You don't want to continually be in the hustle, I assure you.

Perfecting the Love Hustle Toward the Flow of Fun, Joy, and Prosperity. Stop Selling, and Start Creating Prosperity!

On some level, every entrepreneur and intrapreneur loves "the game," but "the game" is far different than the hustle.

The hustle is a bit manic. Like "Where is my next check going to come from?" kind of manic. The game is "Who am I going to catch next?" What will I win? "Who am I going to help?" and "How will I prosper?" That is a much more abundant consciousness.

What if you vibrated at easy, fun, and abundantly successful? Well, the universe would send you more!

One of the best bosses I have ever had and by far one of the funnest jobs in Corporate America I have ever had was when I was a corporate director of sales and marketing in Los Angeles. My boss was a Southern California native who grew up surfing as part of his morning routine. I don't mean he occasionally surfed. Jack surfed every single day. Period. He believed that life and business should mimic surfing. The ocean has a natural rhythm to it, and if you were good at surfing, you became one with that rhythm. You let it become your rhythm, and the flow just happened. Jack wasn't just good at surfing; he was great at it.

He truly believed that all things had their natural and intuitive rhythm, and business and the people who created that business were no different. Jack didn't believe in the old school ways of motivating the sales force through slamming budgets and forecasts down on the table and saying, "Do better." He actually did something that I loved, the controller despised, and was amazingly successful for the company every single year.

In the traditional paradigm, the sales, marketing, and finance departments grind out a budget based on forecasting and revenue histories. Then when all are in agreement, the budget is given to the sales and marketing department who then writes the marketing plan, outlining in great detail what they will do to bring in the numbers that have been committed to on paper. If you have ever been on any side of this exercise, you know it is the most tedious and least abundant practice you can do to gain clairvoyance for the year ahead.

Jack created a new framework and paradigm. He and the controller looked over business history, future trends, and what was already real time business for the upcoming year, and they would come up with a preliminary budget.

Only then would he come to my team and say, "Here is the money that we would like to give you to bring us business. You get to tell us what you want to do in the year that is creative and fun to drive business, and you get to tell us based on the money we are giving you to spend how much business you will bring us in the next year." *Pow!* Marketing and sales love the words "creative," "fun," and "Here is some cash!"

Not only did he give us carte blanche in creating and committing to what we were going to do but he also sent us off to a wonderful beachside hotel to get our abundant creative juices flowing.

You know what this resulted in every single year? We would inevitably come back from our mini beach getaway committing to way bigger goals, revenues, and achievements than anyone ever expected. We were also 100% confident as a team that we could make the numbers we proposed.

Do you know why this worked year after year? Because we were vibrating at joy and abundance, sitting beachside writing our creative, fun, and wildly prosperous marketing plan rather than coming at it through the contraction of fear, overwhelm, or just plain annoyance at the not so zen like controller.

After we committed, all departments would sit down together and add beautiful, wonderful dollars to the revenue forecast. That is exactly what I mean by the Love Hustle! The bast part of all of this was that throughout the year, we got to keep the commitments to having fun and being creative to drive business and revenues. When you are always sitting in the vibration of abundance, you cannot help but create it.

The Love Affair Between Entrepreneurs and Desperation—Break It Off Now!

I don't care if you are sitting up in your blissful Creative entrepreneurial consciousness tower or laying in the gutter of the Can't consciousness, every single entrepreneur one time or another gets a little desperate. That is normal. What you want to avoid is that desperation becoming a base line vibration for you or, even worse, a strategy in which you get business.

When I was in sales, I adored it! I could strategize to have contracts go out and come in with such precision that meeting my numbers and securing accounts were a blast. The busier I was, the more I enjoyed adding more sales calls, dinners, and client evens. It was when I was the most inspired to create amazing experiences for my prospective clients, and all of that brings in business and income!

If I could give you some life changing advice around making sales, it would be make those sales calls when you are busy! But in that all too familiar entrepreneurial panic, we tend to reach out when we are feeling our absolutely lowest and try to drum up business. I hate to break it to you, but you are a vibrational human. When you are vibrating at no business, the universe is going to give you more of the same.

Most entrepreneurs are either running around like a chicken with their head cut off because they are so busy or freaking out because the sounds of the headless hens just became crickets and all signs of business are gone!

That is because most of the time as entrepreneurs, we haven't laid our framework of human balance, let alone the balance of our spirit. When we are busy, we are thinking about how we have to slow down to create that balance, but when things do slow down, panic sets in. We have a knee jerk reaction to create busy because the old paradigm says that if we are busy, we are making money. However, if we took the extra time to create our framework of balance, we would make money easier, faster, and without the fear that comes with slow times. The new paradigm says that when we take advantage of our slow time and acknowledge the prosperity in it, we are still vibrating at prosperity, so the universe delivers more prosperity.

Busting Through Limiting Beliefs Around Creating Income and Receiving Money

Everyone, and I mean everyone, has that moment when they have to put a price tag on what they are doing in the world. This is the single hardest thing we do as business people. Unless you are in a predetermined industry of a specific product, you have to have worth around your business and sometimes around you. This contraction around worth doesn't escape anyone. For some of us, it is a mild hesitation in pricing, and others suffer from complete anxiety when putting a value on their personal services. If we have self-worth issues, we most definitely have business worth issues.

I once saw an amazing leader in the women's health industry speak. She told a story from very early in her career when she was figuring out what she would charge her clients. She would put various rates written on pieces of paper in envelopes. When she booked her client, she would then randomly pick an envelope, open it, and charge that particular client that amount. Brilliance!

Yep, I know what your thinking...that sounds really airy fairy and not a professional way to do business at all. Well, I believe that it is utterly brilliant for many reasons, but here are the top two:

1. This is an intuitive practice, and as spirits in bodies, we are fiercely intuitive. When we honor our intuition, our life becomes easy and abundant.
2. When you do what she did, you actually trick your ego about your self-worth.

When I teach manifesting to my clients, the very first thing I teach is how to trick the ego so that it doesn't get threatened and shut down all of the fun. This practice of picking envelopes lets the ego know that nothing serious is going on so that it can go back to what it was doing, and all is safe in the ego's scary little small world. I mean, who wants your ego hanging around and lecturing you on how you are not worth $500 per hour or how discounting a client to $25 will surely send you to the poor house?

She didn't have to do the envelope game for long before she became clear on her path and the prosperity she was meant for. The important thing is that she created an acceptable way to ask for money until she got the clarity she needed.

Flexing Your Income Muscle: Changing Your Vibration Around Income

A man named Chris came to see me a few years ago. A business that he had started a few years earlier and had had great success with at first had all but drizzled down the drain. In reviewing his business strategy for the past few years, Chris told me that one of the sure fire techniques to get orders was to call clients when business was slow and see if they could help him out. He would start off the call with "Hey, I have a favor to ask," then "I am a little slow, so I thought I would reach out and drum up some business. So, if you are going to be reordering your products, could you help me out?" *It is not our client's job to help us out!*

This seemed to work in the first year, but he came at these sales calls in utter lack. He used it as a strategy, so he continued to find himself in lack. His clients got tired of bailing him out, so they went away. He had felt his clients pull away, but Chris struggled with taking responsibility for himself. Ultimately, having clairvoyance around the fact that clients were leaving because of him was a completely new awareness he had to come to terms with.

In our first plan of attack, I had Chris send out a thank you letter to all of those clients, telling them how grateful he was for the relationship they had and how his business wouldn't be as successful as it was if it weren't for them in those early years. He didn't extend any business discounts or gifts because this was just a letter to hold gratitude, clear up some business karma, and renew his business energy. It was important for him to say those things without making it a business strategy.

The other thing that letter did was give Chris a declaration that his business was a success. I explained to Chris that he was exactly where he was supposed to be based on his entrepreneurial consciousness, habits, and the vibration he held. He should see this situation as a doorway to a very successful rest of his life.

Then in order to shift Chris's awareness from creating income from his clients (which is limited) to creating income, I gave Chris the following exercise from an amazing book, *The Magic* by Rhonda Byrne.

I sent him to get a small journal, and from that day on for the next month, he was to keep this journal with him wherever he went. Whenever someone invited him for coffee or a beer and he didn't go, he was to write down what that would have costed him and record it as income. After the recorded entry, he was to write "Thank you" next to the item. He was to do this for every single money item in his life. So, if he saved $2.00 on peaches, he recorded $2.00 as income, and next to it, he wrote "Thank you" and so on. Chris loved this exercise so much that he recruited his wife. They would sit down every Friday evening and go over all of the income they had made for the week. They made a fun experience of it.

The most amazing thing happens when you do this: you shift into an entirely new awareness of how income can come to you. We are so set in the limiting belief that income can only come from our jobs or business, when in reality, income is any money that is coming in to our life.

In only sixty days of Chris and his wife shifting into this new vibration, two amazing things happened: Chris's business started picking up, and his wife received a long over due promotion and increased her income and the family's household income by over $50,000 annually.

I am sure that by now you are really tired of hearing me say this, but...

The universe simply gives you more of the vibe you are putting out. The universe doesn't judge or try to understand. So, repeat after me: *the universe simply matches the vibes we are laying down!*

It is never—and I do mean never—-the other way around. We are not reacting to what the universe is delivering; the universe is delivering what we are thinking, saying, and focusing on!

When you embrace busy and get really clear on how that busyness is prospering you or not, you can make shifts, and those shifts will create balance.

Generating Business Is Different Than Generating Income

In creating success in your business, you have to hold two aligned yet different realizations: 1) generating business is different than generating income, and 2) you can generate income without generating busyness.

So, the next time you don't have time to generate business, generate it any way. Here is how:

When you are really really slammed, pull your bleary-eyed self up by the boot straps and give a couple of clients or prospective clients a call and tell them "Hey, business is really in a great flow right now, and I am thinking about you. I just want you to know that if you need anything, I am never too busy for you," or "Hey, dude. We are rockin' and rollin' down here, and I can't get you off my mind. If you need anything, you know I am happy to add your project's energy to the mix."

I promise that if you make even one of those calls a day when you are busy, you will have a steadier stream of business throughout the year and be able to hire support so that you are never bleary-eyed again. That is spiritual balance, ease, and flow! In addition, the clients and business you attract will be more aligned with you and the business you are trying to achieve: a positive and abundant one!

When you pull out of the manic vibration of the hustle and move into the flow of fun, joy, and prosperity, you have entered the love hustle, and that energy isn't exhaustive, stressful, or depleting. You are able to sustain a higher energy and brain power for creating a framework to support the dream of your business.

CHAPTER 9

The Spiritual Practice of Divine Communication and Compensation

This is a bit tricky, and that is because as business owners who are "doing it all" or still in a "solopreneur mindset," we are keenly aware of every dollar that is billed and owed. If you do it right, that awareness in and of itself is a superpower. If you are a business owner who is brave enough to look at your bank balance and P&L's every day and has financial clairvoyance, you are a total rockstar! Now, to take it up a notch, no matter how tightly clenched your stomach is, pull up that online banking, and as you do, repeat the following affirmation out loud for three minutes.

"My wonderful life is happy, healthy, wealthy, and safe."

You will literally be able to feel yourself relax no matter what the numbers are. At first, that little voice in your head will be saying, "Oh, yeah? That's crap! Look. You're poor!" Just keep going. Our subconscious is a slave to our words, and as the slave, it creates the knee jerk reactions and behaviors that keep us in fear and self-judgement.

The subconscious's only job is to make what you say right 100% of the time, so if you are looking at a negative number but saying your mantra, you will start feeling and vibrating at happy, healthy, wealthy, and safe. Then you will live it. I promise!

Providing what you do in the world is wildly sacred, and being compensated for what you do is as well. So, the ritual around it should be a high vibrating one.

I know, I know. You are not ritualistic! Well, I beg to differ. Do you grab a cup of coffee on your way to work every day? Do you then get to work and turn on all of the lights or open up windows to let light into your space? Do you return emails and write some of your own? Do you send out monthly invoices? Those are all rituals, and they are important. You are important, and your business is important. So, make everything a special event, especially when it comes to your abundance!

Your Invoices, the Love Letter

The most important forms of divine communication are by far the contract, the solicitation letter, and the invoice. We are such a disconnected society that we mindlessly send out automated everything these days. Long gone are the days of personalized communication. We rely on list builders, electronic documents, and automated invoicing. We have attempted the illusion of personal communication to create sacred compensation, and quite frankly, it is efficient but not a sustainable practice for success.

I love that most of us are all about going green and keeping our communication nice and tidy in online storage systems, but the downside to all of it is energetic disconnect. We cannot attempt to bring in spiritually or consciously aligned business if we schedule everything to happen or if we send our energy half way across the world doing something totally unrelated. It just won't add up energetically. So, here is something that I find to be the second most important spiritual practice of all of the practices: your love letter, the invoice.

Your invoice is the request that you put out into the universe and to your client requesting prosperity for doing what you do for them, so make it count. Do more than make it count. Make it a love letter. This is the document that will set the energy of how fast you get paid. It's vital you do it right. Yes, you have preformed a service and are "owed" the money, but that is not where you should be coming from in your initial invoicing. I don't have a single client who I have had to invoice a second time. You and only you create the speed in which you get paid. Remember, you are creating a magnet with your thoughts and words.

I want you to think back to when your client hired you. You were so excited that the universe had bestowed a new client on you, and that piece of business resulted in added income for you and your business. Now, all of the sudden, wearing your accounts receivable hat and sending out invoices becomes a drudgery that you have to put up with as part of running your own business. It is in that shift where things can get dicey. You see, you have shifted from prosperity and gratitude to annoyance, boredom, and drudgery. When you send out your request for money holding the latter vibration, it slows up the entire process.

Worse than that is when you procrastinate in the accounts receivable portion of your job or when you have a bookkeeper who isn't aligned in gratitude, prosperity, and the Law of Attraction (that discussion is coming up), and the invoices get sent out late. You have set up energetic standard operation procedures that say, "Hey, this money and prosperity just isn't important to me." Yep, you will never be paid on time because you are telling both your client and the universe that you just don't care.

Here is a remedy for the seemingly benign chore of asking for money. Whatever invoices system you have set up, I want you to go into the template, and if your template doesn't have a place for a note, I want you to create one. It doesn't have to be huge, but it does have to have enough space for a nice, beautifully written note.

Address the note to the person who signed the contract and the accounts payable department. Do not do this the other way around. It is important for the flow of energy, I promise. Then you begin by telling them how honored you are to serve them in the way you do, that you know that this will be such a successful endeavor, and that you are grateful for the entire experience with them. Note: This is not where you put the terms of payment. That is a separate portion.

Then send the invoice to both the contract signer and the accounts payable equally, no cc'ing. This creates an equal energy between then person who you created the relationship with and the person who will be holding the financial energy in the partnership.

Why It's Taking So Long to Get Paid and How Spiritual Visualization Can Change That for Good

Our outstanding accounts receivable is a magnetic energy force of money and goodness coming to us for doing something wonderful for someone. We as entrepreneurs make a huge mistake in how we look at our accounts receivable. We spend way too much time watching days pass, getting more and more stressed out, and slipping into the story of "Are they ever going to pay? Are they going to skip out on this bill?" Blah, blah, blah...We get all wadded up because we are engaging in the love affair between the entrepreneur and desperation. Sitting in this vibration of lack and concentrating on the money not coming to you will only keep more money and opportunities from coming to you too. Don't do it!

We are sitting in a vibration of "Why aren't my clients paying their bills?" when we need to be sitting in the vibration that money is coming to us, but only when it collects more.

One of the ways that I pass the time between invoicing and payment received is to imagine it gaining momentum and bringing the prosperity of opportunity to me upon it's arrival.

Let yourself relax and imagine this visualization if you will.

I want you to imagine all of your outstanding accounts receivables as checks or cash just floating out in the universe on their way to you. As they come toward you, they have become magnetized and are attracting more magnetic money and opportunities to you in the form of more clients or additional cash. Wouldn't that be amazing?Because by now, you are well versed in living in creation, intention, and expansion, and you know that is exactly how things work in the world of the Universal Laws.

Isn't it far better to live with the intention that your money owed is bringing you even more in the journey, and the longer it takes to get to you, the more money and opportunity it is bringing too you? Of course it is!

Remember what I said earlier about the vibration of play? When we sit in the vibration of play, we trick our ego into thinking that this new way of being is just a game and nothing to get too serious about or try to control. The vibration of play and joy bring your receivables to you faster than if you are sitting at your computer and watching the days pass as you put all of your attention on the money not in the mail or the bank. Remember, the area where we put our attention grows!

How You Pay Is How You Will Get Paid

Let's face it. We live in a world where we can easily detach from how we personally do things. With social media and the internet, we can easily only give thought processes and awareness to the illusion of how we are and how we do things. Additionally, we adopt what seems to work for so many, which is to aways look at what is newer, trendier, and better.

But when it comes to business practices, especially the expectations of your client's business practices, you need to look no farther than at your own business practices. Yep, folks. Business karma is real, and you can take webinars on generating clients who pay their bills inside of thirty days all you want, but if you don't, they won't! It is the Universal Law of Like Attracts Like. When you stall you are merely sending out a vibration of stalling, you get it right back at you.

So, take a minute and just sit in the awareness of you paying your bills. How does it go? Is it timely and efficient, and do you prosper others easily? Or do you struggle to open your mail? Let it sit on your desk for a few days, and then at the last minute, give up the greens through tightly clenched fists. This is a huge indicator of the energy you hold in the flow of money into your life. If you are a poor exhaler, you cannot possibly be a successful inhaler. Your business's accounting is a rhythm just as breathing is.

Allow the Inhale and Even the Gasp!

Not only do we inhale and exhale prosperity but our clients do also. Let's just assume that they haven't read this book (go buy them one now). That means that they do not have an awareness of the exhale prosperity to inhale prosperity awareness. So, we must allow our clients to open our invoices and inhale deeply. Heck, they might even gasp. That is okay and always allowed. Because when someone inhales, they always exhale eventually. This is why your love letter is so very important. It softens the blow, but what it really does is remind your client of *you* and what you have provided. It is the gift of connection that you have upleveled to in your new invoicing system.

If you as an entrepreneur are focusing on what isn't coming to you, the universe will make you right, and you will have such a hard time receiving money from clients. What we put our attention on grows.

One last thought on communication. What is your communication style? This is an important indicator of how you see your prosperity and how you make your clients feel. Communication is sacred. It is how you inspire clients, colleagues, and people in the world. When we are in defense mode in our communications with people, they feel that energy and almost always react accordingly, which is to distance themselves as opposed to lean in and connect.

A perfect example of this is when you send out a newsletter. Sales funnels are run on mailing lists and customer correspondence. We see something we like, and we sign up for the mailing list without much thought of the other ten newsletters we already receive in a day. We are inundated with offers, newsletters, and videos. The email marketing services industry has become proactive in the retainment of subscribers for their clients. One of these ways is to remind clients why they are receiving this communication. This is detrimental, and nothing says defensive like an opening line in an email saying, "Hey, you asked for this."

Do yourself the biggest favor right now. Change all of your automation reminders to read something along the lines of "Hey, you are getting this because I think you are wonderful, and I appreciate you." *Pow!* This says, "I'm confident, I am coming from an authentic place, and I value you!"

Mailing should never make your client feel like they are being reminded that they value you.

CHAPTER 10

The Energy of Your Employees: Their Limiting Beliefs and Your Success

Your employees are your internal clients, so the Business heart applies!

This chapter is going to be short and sweet. If you are lucky enough to have gotten to the prosperous place where you have employees, reading this book should be an interesting experience for you as you become aware of the entrepreneurial consciousnesses that you have surrounded yourself with.

You may think that the consciousness of your team doesn't matter, that you are the only one who should worry about the vibration you hold. You are wrong. Each person you bring into your company holds a consciousness and a vibration. Based on their position in the company and role with your clients, it is vital that they are showing up every day in the highest expression of their happiness, joy, and love. This is no easy task, I will admit. But I will tell you, at the very least, you should know their beliefs and consciousness around the Business Heart and income.

Your employees are the keys to your kingdom, and because you hired them, it is easy to assume that you felt they were a good fit and able to be an ambassador for you and your dream in the highest of consciousnesses.

Let's take accounts receivable as an example. This is a vital role in an expanded consciousness company in the manifestation of prosperity and abundance for clients, employees, and you. If you have a person who dwells in the vibration of lack handling your money matters, you are setting yourself up for disaster.

You would never hire a sales force that didn't believe in your product. So, why should you hire people who don't have consciousness around the path of your product or what you do in the world?

Am I saying put your employees through the third degree on spirituality and their beliefs in the Universal Laws? Absolutely not. Remember, we are all spirits, and like attracts like. So, if you yourself hold the awareness of the consciousness and vibration of your business, you will surely only hire people who are aligned with you and your dream. Easy rule: *Do not hire people whom you do not love!* They are your internal customers, and you should be working from the three prosperity chambers of your Business Heart with your internal customers as well! It doesn't take an employee to screw things up. Here is an amazing story for you of how I screwed up royally!

Never Leave Off a Zero!

By now, you know that I take this framework seriously. There is no other business model than a totally aligned spiritual one that can succeed on this level. I believe it 100%. Now, through this unfailing belief, I have had some unfortunate examples show up in my business. Are they coincidence? No. Are they manifestations? I believe they are.

A few years ago, I started a passive income generator project. If you have ever heard me speak, you know that I believe that passive income generators are the entrepreneur's retirement package. I have created a few, but by far, this was the best one I had ever created. My goals were really aggressive, and I knew that I could, with some very dedicated work, pull off my goals with ease and success. Two things happened to align the stars not in my favor.

One, when I created this project, I was extremely emotional because this project was a personal one, inspired by someone I loved who was hurting. So, I set the intention that the success of this was so important that I would leverage everything to birth this bad boy into the world! (Don't ever, ever say you will leverage everything for something else!) Of course, I didn't ever think that I would need to leverage anything, let alone everything. I had start up capital, I was aligned with everything and person I needed to be aligned with, and most of it was already done. It was a rewrite. But an intention is an intention, and I had even written it down. Remember when I spoke about the power of writing a goal and intention? Well, I have lived the power.

The other thing I did was that when setting up passwords and logins for each new project, I created my passwords that were a one- or two-word intention tied into a number goal.

For example: Passive$100K would be a password for something that was tied to a passive income goal I was going to achieve in a year. The problem was that when I created my passwords, I left off a zero in each. I clearly was not paying attention and found it during the launch. I meant to go back and change it but never did.

As we were in production, things started to happen completely out of the blue: cars started breaking down, our dishwasher needed to be replaced, and expenses started sky rocketing faster than income was coming in. I ended up going into my savings to finance the project. I realized in the midst of what felt like leveraging everything, I had set a very powerful intention of doing just that.

In that moment, the project almost came to a complete stand still. Luckily, it didn't, and I was able to recalibrate and rectify to feel strong and secure, but many months had passed that I just couldn't get back.

Admittedly, I was disappointed for not hitting my financial goals in the first year, but in cleaning up all of the old emails from the project, I came across one about my project login information. The most amazing thing happened; the revenue I made was the exact number I used in my login password. My goal was shy on one very important zero at the end.

CHAPTER 11

The 20/80 Rule: Lie Number Three and Living in Creation, Visualization, Intention, and Expansion

To be successful as an entrepreneur, you must prepare your days to be successful. I know you are probably thinking, "Yes, I know: goals, actions plan, marketing plans, etc." That is not what I mean. What I am talking about is the emotional, mental, and spiritual side of planning.

When I say close your eyes and picture success, many people see a large bank balance. What I actually mean is close your eyes and watch your life on a screen in front of you. Where are you? What do your day to day practices, routines, and rituals look like? Not only do you need goals, objectives, and action plans but you also need to state and prepare for success, and that means preparing for what both your personal and business life look like being successful. This is where the 20/80 rule comes in to play.

The 20%/80% Rule

Practical actions should make up 20% of your day, and spiritual actions should make up the other 80%. Practical actions are what you state must happen, such as goals, action plans, sales, accounts receivable, etc., and spiritual actions are the preparations you make in the expansion of your experience on this earth and in your business. When you spend 80% in preparation for this nature, it only takes 20% to achieve skyrocketing success!

When you create goals and action plans, you are creating a statement of exactly what you will do to achieve a specific end result. When you set intentions for your days, weeks, and months, you are preparing to set the vibration through expansion to support the energy of your end result. When you set intention for your year, you have built a strong structure for your goals to be achieved. Your goals change through out the year based on circumstances, but intentions never do. Intentions are how we live.

Remember that in the introduction I told you about the three lies and said lie number three was coming later in the book? Well, here is lie number three: we can only make income from the 20%. I am so happy to report that I have seen over and over again that we can and do make money from the 80%.

20% Practical Practices

- Business Development
- Account Management
- Accounts Receivable/Payable

- Budgeting/Forecasting
- Marketing/Sales
- Tech Development

The 20% needs no further explanation. It is what we have been raised to believe is the way we make money. We grow up and get jobs without the consciousness that we need to live as a being whose birthright is ease, flow, and prosperity in all things.

80% Spiritual Practices

Who you are:
When you sit in the clarity of who you really are and what your own prosperity is, you are best able to create practices that align with the truth within you.

What you love:
When you create a business based on love and surround yourself with people whom you love, you are inspired and not exhausted. You have expansion in creativity and all things prosperous.

Perfecting your 80%

Aligning your business practices with the above is the practice of living through creation, visualization, intention, and expansion. Let me break it down for you further.

The Four Energies

Creation

We are all creative. Now, if you are analytical, that throws you, right? From the second we wake up in the morning to the moment we close our eyes, we are creating. Our subconscious even creates through dreams while we sleep. We are a tireless creative machine!

When we sit in creation, we are sitting in the endless power of who we are and what we want. When you sit in the conscious energy of creation, you are not going about your day in an unconscious manner; you are planning how things will go in your day, your year, and your life. When we are young, we look to the future and say, "This is what my adulthood will look like," and that is creating. When we create a business, we are planning our business future. When that business is part of a bigger, more abundant, and happy life plan, then we expand into a bigger creative energy, and that creates magic.

How do we create?

We create through both our imagination and our mindset of organization. Our imagination creates the big picture through visualization, and then our organizational mindset takes the dream and gives it detail, the hows through setting, intentions, and planning.

To create income and success through the conscious energy of creation is to step forward in what I like to call the Prosperity of Possibility. When we sit in the energy of creating the Prosperity of Possibility, we expand to our very highest self. When business is conducted through our very highest self, we not only change and prosper ourselves but we also prosper the world.

Visualization

From the time we were little, we were visualizing. If you are sitting there thinking that you can't visualize, then I want you to close your eyes and picture an apple. Now, picture the room you are sitting in. That is visualization. Most people say that they cannot visualize their dreams when what they really mean is they are unclear what they want in life. This is merely due to a disconnection to the truth of who they really are.

When someone begins working with me, the first thing I assign them to is creating a dream life plan. More than an outline, this document is a creative brain dump that is either in story form or an actual mapping out of their life using circles, squares, and connecting lines. It is easier for people to feel that they are just dreaming and imagining in this way than creating a document that they will be held accountable for. What transpires without the pressure to preform is a full life creation of joy and prosperity in all things as opposed to singled out sections of objectives and action plans.

When you have your dream life down in whatever form it takes, you then can set to work on vision boards, visualization meditation, and such. When you don't do this, things get lost in the mix of creation and visualization. You must let the organizational system of your brain in on the game so that nothing is forgotten, and you create a subconscious block to your goals and abundance.

Here is a perfect example of what I am talking about:

Your visualizing yourself as a successful entrepreneur, and one of the components is that you are thinner as a successful person. (This is a very common correlation with success.)

This is an awesome way to work on healthy habits. However, there is a downside to this, and that is that the weight element can actually block you from prosperity and success. If the visualization of you thinner is just that, then what you are telling your subconscious is "As long as I look like this, I am not successful." The purpose of visualizing yourself the way you like during manifesting success is to create positive vibrations around actually being successful. So, I would recommend that you recreate a visualization and imagine you professionally successful and happy exactly how you are right now. The upside to that is it actually doesn't put any obstacles or conditions between you and success like my client Kate did.

A year ago, a lovely woman named Kate contacted me to do some work with her around changing her vibration and manifesting her dream life. As she put it, she had come up against a wall in manifesting the final outcome of success that she had visualized for so long. Where most of the pieces had seemingly fallen into place, she just couldn't get to the place where it all came together for her.

She admitted that she was having a hard time with "feeling" successful and prosperous. She would get really excited when one of her goals were met, but she would look in the mirror that night and feel like it was just another day and nothing had changed.

When I went to her office, I saw affirmations, inspirational art on the walls, and a vision board. The vision board was filled with wonderful photos of exotic places, money, a couple on the beach, and a house in the mountains. It had phrases like "ease and flow," "wealth," "happiness," "love," and "CEO" (which, if rumors were accurate, that was coming soon.)

At least 75% of the images had manifested into reality for her. She had a wonderful relationship, they took vacations to exotic places, and she made amazing money, but she still couldn't finalize the last few and really important goals.

I put Kate into a deep meditation where she walked through a typical perfect day in her new dream life from morning to night.

As she woke up and took a shower, everything seemed normal, then she went to her closet and pulled out a size two dress and slipped it on. There it was, the incongruity that we were missing.

I let her continue through the visualization, and when she came out of meditation, I asked, "So, when you see yourself in your dream life you are seeing yourself physically looking thinner?" She replied, "Yes, when I have achieved all of my goals, I will be my ideal weight and shape."

I looked around, and there was nothing on her vision board about health or working out. There was nothing in her dream life plan she sent me that indicated losing weight was a focus, and no goals had ever been set around her health at all. When I asked Kate about this, she was amazed. She said that she never thought about it except for when she imagined herself with everything she wanted, she was skinny. She saw the disconnect.

She was unable to hit the right vibration to attract success because when she looked in the mirror every day, she saw herself a she was, not a skinny version of her, so she never felt like her dreams were manifesting. Her reflection was a subconscious trigger that she hadn't made progress, so she was always frustrated. That night, she went back to her dream life business plan and her vision board and added health to both. She incorporated the activities to both her daily routine and visualizations that supported losing weight.

When she shifted her awareness around how powerful her subconscious was and worked with it, she began to achieve her health goals too. Within six months, she had gotten a CEO position and was well on her way to a slimmer version of her happiest self. The best part is that Kate realized that being happy didn't actually have much to do with her losing weight at all.

When you are visualizing something as important as your successful business and income, it is imperative that you be thorough in the organization structure of how. Even if you do not notice small inconsistencies, your subconscious does, and it's only job is to make you right.

Intentions

When we live through the awareness that we create our reality and life doesn't throw things at us that do, we are living in the awareness of intention. When we begin our days with setting intentions, we claim our space in the experience that is going to go exactly how we want. We don't leave room for boredom, negativity, and stress unless that is what you are intending.

Every day, I start my day out with an amazing visualization, and I want to teach it to you. By now, you have created a sacred space in which to do the work that you need to do. Whether that is a special room, somewhere outside, or your office, you should be spending your time in creation, visualization, intention, and expansion in this space.

I want you to hold your two hands out in front of you as if you are holding a basketball. Your hands should be facing each other. Now, imagine that you have a beautiful clear sphere in your hands. This symbolizes your day. Outside of this sphere are words, phrases, people, and the intentions you want to include in your day. Also, notice that in the outer edges of these words and phrases are words with negative condensations like *hard*, *stressful*, *poor*, and *fail*. As you watch your galaxy of both positive and negative words and phrases, I want you to imagine reaching out, plucking your choices from the orbit, and adding them to your sphere.

Notice how you would never consciously put the words *stress*, *failure*, or *difficult* into your sphere, so why do we unconsciously add it to our days? Most of us believe that stress, difficulty, and failure happen to us. This isn't true. When you run your business through setting intentions in this way, you are living purposefully, and when we do that, we are claiming our success.

Another effective way to run your business and life through intention is the day planner effect. Most of our calendars are synced up to phones, desktops, laptops, and tablets, and that is just fine for the purpose of setting your appointments, but there is a way to use analog calendars for the good of your day.

Yes, it needs to be written in a book. This is a sacred practice and needs to be held in high regard.

I want you to purchase a large 8.5x11 weekly planner. The weekly planners have the generous space that you will need.

Every morning, set four or five intentions on how you want to move forward in your day. Write larger than usual and make sure to leave space at the bottom. At the end of your day, open up your planner and write how your intentions manifested. It doesn't need to be a lengthy entry, just a sentence. The important thing here is that you get to see the fruits of your intentions appear in front of you.

Creation

Living in the Highest Expression of Expansion

When our thoughts, agreements, and beliefs are in alignment, we are mentally aligned with our path, and when we are walking our truest and highest path and set out to change life for just one person, we are succeeding spiritually, abundantly, and joyfully. That's when we change the world. That is living in expansion.

The first three energies are the practices and ways of being that create expansion in the energy of who you are. When we live in an expanded awareness of our spirit, creation, visualization, and intentions become our way of life.

The other component of expansion is knowing ourselves fully. Can we ever really know ourselves fully? I think so. At least, we can on the journey we are on in that given moment. In all of my years working with people, the biggest challenge for people is looking deeply inward and knowing what they truly believe in as opposed to what they agree with.

In the depths of who we are, we have two systems; one is our agreement system, and the other is our belief system.

An agreement system is when you listen, see something in the world, or are taught something and say, "Yes! That resonates deeply, and I want to take that on." In other words, that "feels" like you. So, you agree with it deeply. This is what communities, cultures, and tribes are built upon,. Agreement feels exactly like a belief, but it's different.

A belief system is when we are sitting alone and going deep into the truth of who we are, and the only influence we have is our thoughts aligned with the golden current of our heart. That's when we experience the feeling of deep expansion in our being.

When other's belief systems are in line with our own beliefs, that is when we are walking the path of who we really are, and we are able to show up true in the world. We are walking the path of spirit when we have true relationships and experiences.

When we are sitting in a lower vibration due to stress, perceived failure, and disappointment, we become stuck and eventually paralyzed, unable to move forward. The Can't Consciousness knows all about this, and it's not fun.

Here is your secret weapon for moving through paralyzation: mantras. Mantras are short affirmations that when you say them over and over, they create change in your subconscious and your vibration. When you say a mantra or affirmation out loud for ten minutes, you say it 250 times. When you do that, you begin to change your cellular structure and neural pathways in your brain. You are literally changing *you*!

If you are feeling stuck, I want you to try it. Below is a list of short mantras that work wonders. Make sure though that you say this out loud every single day for thirty days. At first, you might feel like you are lying, or you might feel silly. Keep going. Soon, you will be shocked at how you are looking at the world. You will start to notice the positives and the ability you have to forge ahead.

- Everything always works out for me.
- I move forward in confidence and ease
- I have everything I need to succeed
- I prosper in everything I do.
- I am successful in everything I do.

Have fun, and remember, our subconscious is the slave to the words we say. It's only job is to make us right, so it would be wonderful if we were feeding it the good stuff!

Balancing Your Human and Your Being as a Leader

As we all know, there are many different types of leaders, but they really break down into only two categories: the Human Leader and the Being Leader.

We are a combination of two energies. Our first energy is our Human Energy, which is the body, the "what we do" in this world, and the "I'm only human." It is our physical self and our baseline belief system (the one we don't know why we believe it, and quite possibly, deep down inside, we don't even know if we agree with it). This is the part of us that is powerful in getting things done, making success stories out of our lives, and taking charge of all things. But when we are not in balance and the human energy is too dominant, we get stuck and just can't move forward.

Then, there is your Being Energy. This is our higher self that is ruled by intuition, creativity, and a deeper sense of self-knowledge and Universal Truths. This is the part of us that sees the big picture, gets overwhelmed by details, and has the ability to get derailed and even paralyzed in actualizing the dream. When we find ourselves floating around in la la land, not relating to anyone and not grounded into the moment, we are living in our Being, and that is when we tend to go into "I am an island" mode.

More often than not, one of our sides has raised the white flag and surrendered to the other side, and we live out of balance. The idea of our life and work here is to balance these two sides and live and lead fully in your Human Being. When we actively live and lead in our Human Being, we become an unstoppable force to be reckoned with. It's powerful and easy.

The aligned Human Being leader is both comfortable with goals and action plans as well as coming from the awareness of Universal Laws and spiritual practices. I am including a practice to align your Human and your Being in the exercise section in the back of the book. It has changed my life and the lives of the many clients who have adopted it.

My Letter to the Universe Story

When I first moved to Northern California and was going through my divorce, I opened up a small organic eatery and catering company. But as time went on and I was no longer in my transition, I hung my shingle as a medium and promptly closed up shop to follow my dream. I had all of the money I needed to create a safe place in which to do this, but soon after, a financial agreement I was in ended. Suddenly, I needed to find an extra $500 a month to cover some commitments that I had made while in the earlier situation.

I sat in meditation and became really clear on what I loved and was grateful for in the world, and then I wrote a contract to the universe. First, I listed all of the things that I loved to do more than anything: being a mom, being a medium, gardening, antiquing, having dinner parties, etc., etc. Then I asked the universe to send me an extra $500 per month, and in return, I would be my absolute highest and happiest self and do all of the things above to the very best of my abilities. It was a job contract of sorts. But my job was only to show up doing the things I loved to do.

So, the next morning, I was standing in line at the doughnut store, and in walked the owner of a winery where I had been storing all of my old catering supplies. He said, "Susan, what are you doing these days? I haven't seen you and still have all of your things." I told him that in that very second, I was getting doughnuts for a bunch of teenage boys (because I was showing up the very best mom I could be on a Saturday). He said, "I want to buy all of your restaurant supplies" and offered up double what I had asked the universe for in cash! I was being my very best self as a mom, and I made money. The universal contract worked!

Every month from that day on, I made double my contracted rate. So, not only did the universe pay me for showing up happy but it also gave me a raise. Now, every October, I do the same thing with my annual income, and then I keep my part of the bargain. As usual, the universe delivers to me what I asked for and more.

CHAPTER 12

Money Isn't Messy; Our Mindset Is

Money Belief Systems: Where They Came From and How to Magically Change Them

There is a single adult who doesn't have to deal with the exchange of money. There is no class you can take in your freshman year of high school that prepares you for it, nor is it like a driver's license where you have to go out with an instructor and pass a test on it. We are just left to what we subconsciously learned or did not learn from our parents. Those same parents didn't have training either, and most likely, they just learned from what they did or didn't see growing up.

If your parent's always said that money is hard to come by, chances are that you believe that as well. If you saw your parents fight over bills and finances, chances are you and your spouse will too. There are many ways that we get our belief system around money and income. For me, it was the time babysitting got weird that created my money mess.

That Time Babysitting Got Weird and How It Created My Original Money Mess

I started babysitting when I was thirteen years old. I was allowed to hang up a flyer on a community board at a local business, and within a few days, a woman who lived on the next street over called me. She had a one year old and worked nights occasionally and needed my help. I started working the next week for her. I was so excited that someone thought I was responsible and grown up enough to watch her baby that I lost sight of the actual reason why I was babysitting in the first place: for money.

The first night she came home and went to pay me the agreed amount, she didn't have cash. She said that she didn't want me to have to cash a check, so she would owe it to me. At thirteen, I was more than happy to agree. I just didn't know any better. Plus, she scheduled a second job before I left, so I was thrilled. Yes, my little thirteen-year-old ego was getting some strokes. I didn't have a car, and my mom provided for us. So, I didn't actually need to be paid, and I didn't want to make a big deal of it.

The woman referred me to friends, and soon, my weekends were filled with babysitting jobs. The only thing was that I was actually owed more money from my clients than I had collected from a year of jobs. So, there began my weird and dysfunctional relationship with income. Flash forward years later to when I was selling my art to beautiful upscale stores in the beach town I lived in as a new mom, I never had problems securing accounts or creating beautiful inventory for my clients, but when it came to invoicing and collecting my money, I just couldn't do it. I was still living in the energy of the money dysfunction I had from those babysitting jobs when I was thirteen.

I hired a friend to be my account receivable and took control of shifting that part of my awareness. Once I saw the money I was making from my "side gig," the block quickly dissipated, and all was good.

For some of us, it's not that easy. The money dysfunction that we get in those early years as young employees or entrepreneurs is critical to our development as a thriving business owner. Take a few minutes and think back to your early days of employment. Can you see any correlations in the belief system you hold around your accounts receivable now?

Time Energy/Money Energy: It's All Energy!

Just like breathing and money hold the same energy flow, the management of time is the same energy as the management of money. If you don't have consciousness around the importance of the hours in your days and how you spend them, you most certainly won't have consciousness around your money and where it ends up going

Show Me Someone Who Struggles with Time Management, and I'll Show You Someone Who Struggles with Money Management.

Recently, I was introduced to a woman who was a pillar in the financial community. She had a spectacular reputation for the consciousness she created for her clients around their finances, and I was thrilled to be asked to collaborate on some projects with her. We had set up a coffee appointment, and I got to the restaurant just before our meeting to get us a table. At about ten minutes after our set time, I texted her to see if everything was okay. I heard nothing. I checked to make sure I had the date and time correct and then checked to see if she had responded back. Still nothing. At twenty minutes after, I said that I would wait ten additional minutes, but then we would have to reschedule.

As I was getting up to leave, she walked in the door, no apology, no reason. She was just late and had absolutely no energy around the fact that that was an issue. I asked her if she had gotten my text, and yes, in fact, she had. But she thought she would be there soon enough and could still get a visit in.

The appointment was soon recovered. She was charming and had some brilliant ideas on how we could work together. I was able to make it clear that in the future, I would not be willing to wait, that one of my absolutes was that meetings were to start on time and end on time, that we had mutual respect for the work that each other put out into the world, and that meant having respect around time constraints.

The next call was via Skype. She showed up to this one stressed and discombobulated. She explained that she had found herself in quite a financial bind. She had been a bit careless in looking at her own finances, and now she was coming up against heavy, unplanned property tax bills and vendor bills. She confided that as fastidious as she was with other people's money, she was exhausted and overwhelmed at paying attention to her own. She had come from a family that as long as she worked and went to school as a young adult, all bills and finances were taken care of. She never learned how to manage her own financial affairs, and in her mid 50's, she still struggled with the responsibility of it all.

I asked her if she was ever held accountable for tardiness and keeping appointments. She laughed and said that she was from generations of tardiness and that being late by a few minutes had nothing to do with the money issues in her life. I explained to her that it wasn't being late that had anything to do with the money issues, but rather the unconsciousness she held around time management that did.

The other correlation that time and money have in common is that when people are chronically late, they suffer from low self-esteem. They don't matter and neither does their attendance at the event, so there is no big hurry to get there. It is the same with money. When you can't manage your money effectively, you are imprinting on your soul that you are not worthy of having an abundance of money and ease and flow with it.

Yes, There Is Enough Time to Do Every Thing You Want to Do Unless You're Choosing to Do What You *Don't* Want to Do!

If you remember in chapter 4, lie one was the lie that we don't have enough time to change. The truth is that we have all the time in the world to do what is important to us. This lie is the number one excuse for someone who doesn't want to change. They promise themselves and the people around them that as soon as things calm down, changes will be made. But things never calm down, and no change is ever made.

The minute a client tells me they don't have enough hours in a day, they get homework. Yes, on top of their already packed out day, I give them thirty days of homework. I assign a mantra that says, "I have all of the time in the world," or "I have more than enough time to get everything done." This is met with eye rolls and guffaws, but they do it. They almost always report back that time just seemed to open up for them somewhere in the two-week period of the month. That is because as they are saying their mantras, their subconscious is recording that phrase as fact. As it records the mantra as fact, it makes it true, opening up both their awareness to time and the schedule and choices to make even more time available.

Summary

We are so lucky to live in the times we are living in right now. We can be anything we want and create anything we want to as an invocation. We are all given the abilty to dream and manifest those dreams into reality equally and abundantly. When we sit in the prosperity of that possibilty, our lives unfold in the highest expression of love and joy.

To believe otherwise is limited in the fact that we are only believing in what can be seen and logically rationalized by the masses. What if we came at life with the pricipals, practices and truths that we are all spirits and our work is our spiritual expression that creates prosperity for all. Wouldn't that open us all up to the beauty and wonder of all that life has to offer.

When we let go of our limiting beliefs around not having enough money, wealth is for others and not us or that wealthy people are bad, we create an entirely new paradigm around the energy of income. We can not show up in the world to affect change on a global level, if we are terrified that we can't pay our mortgage or buy groceries on a personal level.

We will shft the world when we shift where the money comes from and that shift begins with each of us. When we shift the beliefs around money and income from our head which is where stress, fear and greed reside to our hearts which is where love, joy and generosity reside we will change the world.

So, there you have it, the practices, energies, awarenesses, and vibrations you need to hold to change the paradigm for what you do in the world and the prosperity it will bring you. I have worked with thousands of people and have seen amazing things happen in their lives when they follow these new truths. Remember, life isn't supposed to be hard and stressful. It just isn't. Ease and flow are the gifts you are given for stepping onto the path that is your birthright. When you sit in the highest expression of joy, happiness, and love, it is good for you, the people you love, and the world.

You are a spirit in a body, and your business is a spiritual endeavor. Go out and give freely, and then sit in the awareness of how you prosper the world and receive the prosperity from the world in return. You deserve it.

Your Spiritual Practices Exericses and Tool Kit

Attracting Your Perfect Client Worksheet

Step 1: What qualities do I want my perfect _____ to possess and demonstrate?

Compile this list by thinking about things you love about existing or past _____. Choose one or two qualities from each to create your ideal _____.

Questions you can ask to create this list may include:

How do they treat me?
How do they express themselves?
How do they dress?
How do I feel around them?
What qualities, characteristics, attributes and talents do
    they have?

Step 2: What makes my perfect _____ tick?

This is where the magic happens. Step 1 relieved your mind of obvious traits your perfect _____ possesses. Now you can access your creativity and design your relationship with your perfect _____ based on something more solid and fundamental.

The key to creating far more satisfying and synchronistic relationships is to say what usually goes unsaid, to share the motivations and missions that drive us and our perfect _____. What is most important to them in their lives. We will be in a much better place to be available to receive their gifts and give them ours. This is where synchronicity starts.

Write down answers to the following questions about your perfect _____:

Why do they get out of bed in the morning?
Who is the most important person in the world to them?
What is most important to them in the world?
What do they want to achieve before they leave this world?
What do they really love about their life?

A foundation for a great relationship can be set by asking yourself the same questions. Based on the principle that "like attracts like," you can be assured that your most perfect _____ are motivated by the same missions, issues, and challenges that you are.

Creating Your Business heart:

The 3 Prosperity Chambers
of the Business Heart

Take a moment and sit quietly with an awareness of your top clients or perspective clients, ask yourself: Which two chamber does this client fit within? Remember, one MUST always be love.

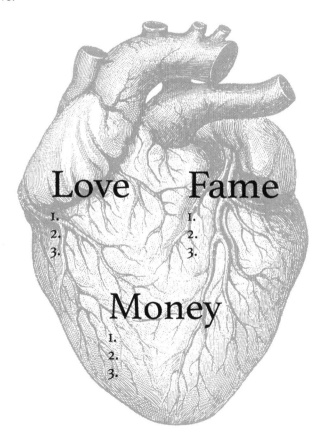

Getting to know your clients and potential clients!

1. Name: _____
    Chamber 1._____Chamber 2._____
    Why_____
    _____

    How can you best show up to honor your client's business in return?_____
    _____
    _____

2. Name: _____
    Chamber 1._____Chamber 2._____
    Why_____
    _____

    How can you best show up to honor your client's business in return?_____
    _____
    _____

3. Name: _____
    Chamber 1._____Chamber 2._____
    Why_____
    _____

How can you best show up to honor your client's business in return?_____

_____

_____

What two Prosperity Chambers does your ideal client dwell in? Why?

Creating your own prosperity pyramid:

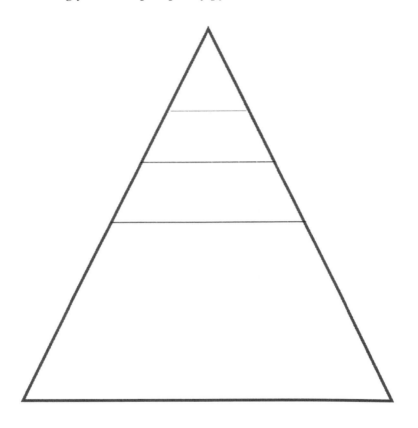

To create clairvoyance around your business, based on what you learned in the workshop, here are some questions that will help you decide the four layers of your prosperity pyramid.

Free:

Who do you want to give to without asking anything in return?
Why? (this can be a person, business or segment)

_____

_____

_____

_____

_____

Trade:

What are the boundaries of your trade segment? For example,
how many a year? to who? worth limit? agreed timeframe?

_____

_____

_____

_____

_____

Discount:

Sit quietly and ask yourself, what do I base giving a discount
for? Support, family, love and exposure?

_____

_____

_____

_____

_____

What discount are you offering?

_____
_____
_____
_____
_____

Income Channels:

Look at all of the different ways you can bring in income, now take some time and list them out with either the amount of time you are willing to dedicate to each one or what business do you want to bring in and how much of each.

_____
_____
_____
_____
_____
_____
_____
_____
_____
_____
_____

Remember, The Universe always prefers to deliver on what you WANT not what you believe you need!

Perfecting your 80% for creating income

<u>Vibration Upleveling</u>

Creating Sacred Space – Meditation – 10 Minute Mantra Work – Physical Care of Your Human – Seeking Laughter and Joy – Drinking Water – Morning Channeling Exercise – Bestowing Prosperity –

<u>Spirit Centered Practice of Gratitude and Thought</u>

This is the space in your day where you sit in quiet, preferably early in the morning.

To hold gratitude for the day you have a head of you as well as the closing of yesterday, you set the vibration of gratitude for your day and when you vibrate at gratitude the Universe delivers more to be grateful for. This is the ideal time for thinking about all of your success'and joys. There isn't anything that will raise your vibration faster than focusing on joys and success.

<u>Visualization/Intention Setting</u>

This is the practice where dreamers get to dream and non dreamers get to plan, because Surprise! they are the same thing!!! Take 10 minutes out of each morning and focus on (and only on) your dream life. Do not get too detailed in what it is you are trying to create. The Universe does not recognize try, it only delivers what we are feeling in that moment, 10 minutes is all it takes. Intention setting is how you control how your day and life goes, when we don't set the intentions for our experiences to manifest, it is easy for days, weeks and life to get away from us. So in this time, connect into the feeling of your visualization, then align your daily intentions to support the creation of your dream life.

Now, let's work on building your 80%
(please use your quiz results from Chapter 2 as a reference.)

How many hours do you work right now?

_____

What is your "Hours a week" goal?

_____

What is your Consciousness vibration?

_____

What is your vibrational goal?

_____

Name 5 upleveling actions that you are willing to commit to daily

Creating Sacred Space - Meditation - 10 Minute Mantra Work - Physical Care of Your Human - Seeking Laughter and Joy - Drinking Water - Aligning your Human and your Being Exercise - Bestowing Prosperity

1._____
2._____

3._____
4._____
5._____

Go a little deeper with how each will look for you

1._____
2._____
3._____
4._____
5._____

What time of day will you commit to your Spirit Centered Practice of Gratitude and Thought?

_____

Where will you commit to doing your Spirit Centered Practice of Gratitude and Thought?

_____

Write down and commit to claim your success! Success is very personal so feel through this exercise. This is what you will build your visualization and intentions off of.

_____
_____
_____
_____
_____
_____

What are the first three intentions that you can set to support and activate your success?

1._____

2._____

3._____

Visualize and Intention setting exercise

Your new daily intention practice - Every morning as you are dressed and ready to begin your day, visualize holding a clear sphere in your hands(like a basketball). It represents the day you have in front of you. Floating around this sphere are words and images that will make up your day as you put them inside.

Here are a few suggestions, remember what happens in your day is a direct result of this practice and the intentions that you set forth to manifest - joy - ease - flow- help - confidence - love - money - success kindness - abundance - laughter - grateful - peace - serenity progress - can - expansiveness - possibilty - magic acknowledgement - happiness - resolve commitment communication - partnership - collaborate - simple - timely alignment - love (that one is always worth saying twice)

I have included the following intentions and words in my sphere_____

_____

_____

_____

_____

_____

Spiritual Practice: Creating Your Success Mindset - Create a stand alone page that you will commit to filling out and live by daily.

1. What five words will define my day?
2. What magic am I expecting today?
3. What 5 things am I most grateful for today?
4. What is the most important change I can make in my life to change everything?
5. What would it take for me to change it?
6. What "Acts of Faith" am I engaging in to tell the Universe that I am ready for success?

How were you your very highest self today?

_____

How were you not?

_____

What will you commit to changing in order to rectify?

_____

Spiritual Practice: Your Contract With the Universe

Dear Universe,

Here is what I love to do most in my time here on earth

_____

_____

_____

_____

_____

_____.

Here is the income that I would like to request, to create abundance in love, happiness, health and safety for myself, my family and the world _____.

I wholeheartedly commit and contract to showing up doing the above as the highest expression of myself and in the highest expression of all the love and happiness that I was born to be. I will engage fully in life with love and gratitude.

For this is my promise to you.

_____

YOU

The Top 3 Practices to Upgrade Your Vibe!

1. When you say a mantra/ affirmation for 10 minutes outloud every day, you are saying it 250 times. At 250 times you literally change your cellular structure and neural pathways. Below are a list of mantras for you to choose from. This is singlehandedly the fastes way to up your vibe!

    1. Everything always works out for me.
    2. Money and Abundance flow freely to me every day in every way.
    3. I have all that I need to succeed right now.
    4. Clients pay me well, for a job well done.
    5. My magnificent life is happy, healthy wealthy and safe.
    6. I move forward with confidence and ease.
    7. I create wealth and prosperity with ease.
    8. I am so grateful for every single thing in my life.
    9. The more fun I have the prosperity I create.
    10. I love and am so grateful for my life.

2. Your History of Happiness! I hope your ready, this is a doozy. On a piece of paper, I want you to think back to when you were 5, okay, if that is too long ago, go back to 10 years old. Write a list of 5 things that brought you utter happiness. Then grow up 5 years and make a list of what made you deleriously happy at 15, keep going until you reach now, and remember, these are items that made YOU happy and brought YOU joy. Not

your family, your friends or your dog, YOU! Lastly, anchor in to this happiness and use it as a compass for happiness now! We are put her to be happy, start now!

3. Stand facing the sunrise, feet flat on the floor and hands at prayer postion with thumbs pressed against the sternum (you are a human arrow shooting up into the Universe) repeat this Universal prayer daily:

"Please make me a channel of Divine creativity, use me as a tool for higher will. I see, I hear and I know!"

Vibrational Upleveling exercise

The 3 awareness' to hold in upleveling: Please sit in a minimum of 3 minutes in each awareness daily.

1. A moment where you have felt bliss.
2. A moment where you felt you were in your highest expression of Joy and Love.
3. A moment that you were filled up and more with gratitude for life.

Bibliography

Hawkins, David R., M.D. Power vs. Force
Sedona, Arizona Veritas Publishing 2001
5th printing, pg. 234

By A. Pawlowski, No cash? No problem, if you barter
CNN U.S. Edition September 2, 2008

http://www.womensmarketing.com/blog/2014/11/
health-and-wellness-market/

Rhonda Byrne, The Secret The Power Atria Books August 2010

Made in the USA
Middletown, DE
04 December 2021